# Grow Your Accounting Practice Using Bill.com

## Improve How Clients Pay, Get Paid, and Manage their Money

Judie McCarthy

Published by

The Sleeter Group

Copyright © 2014

| | |
|---|---|
| Product Name | Grow Your Accounting Practice Using Bill.com: Improve How Clients Pay, Get Paid, and Manage their Money |
| | 2014 |
| | ISBN 978-1-942417-00-2 |
| Trademarks | Bill.com®, Intuit®, QuickBooks™, PracticeMaster, Needles®, TSheets, SpringAhead, BigTime, Sage Timeslips, BillQuick, Tabs3, Time Matters, Billing Matters, Amicus® Attorney, Amicus® Premium Billing, Concur Expense, Expensify, Nexonia, Constant Contact®, SmartVault®, Bill & Pay, Worldox®, and NetDocuments® trademarks or service marks are the property of their respective owners and should be treated as such. |
| Copyright | © 2014 The Sleeter Group, Inc. |
| | All rights reserved |
| | Distilled 11/25/14 12:04 PM |
| | BillCom_Final_Printed_2.docx |
| Disclaimer | This material is intended as a learning aid. Under no circumstances shall the author or publisher be liable for any damages, including any lost profits, lost data, or other indirect damages arising out of anything written in this document or expressed directly or indirectly by the author or publisher. |
| Written By | Judie McCarthy |
| Foreword | Doug Sleeter |

# Table of Contents

# Foreword

As the founder of The Sleeter Group, I have worked for the past twenty years at the intersection of technology and accounting to help CPAs and other accounting professionals understand how to use the best tools for their clients in becoming more efficient and profitable.

Growing an accounting practice depends on leveraging technology such as Bill.com. We have recognized Bill.com with our annual Awesome Application award in three of the past five years, and that achievement is a testament to its excellence in cloud-based accounting.

In this book, Judie McCarthy reveals the world that opens up for accounting professionals and their clients by adopting Bill.com. Ever since I met Judie, I've been impressed by her passion for accounting technology. She shares my view that cloud-based accounting is transforming the accounting field, and is eager to share this new world with other accounting professionals.

Our hope is that this book will help you and your clients be more successful and efficient. We value your input and feedback, so let us know which products you would like us to evaluate. Visit our blog at www.sleeter.com/blog to join the conversation with Judie and the rest of our authors.

*— Doug Sleeter, Founder and President*
*The Sleeter Group*
*October 2014*

# Preface

## How I Got Here

In 2001, long before the cloud revolution, I began my journey of transitioning my client accounting services from on-site to be fully remote. My company utilized common carriers for sending and receiving client paperwork and exchanged data files on floppy disks or CDs.

By eliminating travel time to and from client locations, we would be able to service more clients without adding additional staff. This also presented an opportunity to standardize our processes, which allowed us to become even more efficient. Because this model cut the time it took to complete client work, it only made sense to move from time billing to a fixed-fee model. Back then, our operations seemed like a well-oiled machine, running at maximum efficiency. It just couldn't get any better.

In 2004, I adopted my first cloud technology for processing payroll; this was a game changer. This cloud application allowed me to expand my business by offering remote payroll services without the need to print and mail checks and forms. For clients who used QuickBooks, we could send a file to import their payroll details into their accounting file. Because the monthly subscription fee included all the features, we knew this would fit perfectly into our fixed-fee pricing model.

Remember I just said it couldn't get any better? Well it did!

In 2007, I met Rene Lacerte, founder of Bill.com. Rene introduced me to his new cloud application and asked me to give it a try. He told me that it would change the way businesses pay bills and get paid. Honestly, I was a bit skeptical. But hey, nothing ventured, nothing gained.

## Fast Forward to Today

Using a team of remote talent, my company manages payroll and client accounting services for small businesses from Maine to Miami. Thanks to Bill.com, we can do this by working collaboratively with our clients from anywhere, without the need to touch paper, print checks, or stuff envelopes. We use either cloud-based or hosted accounting solutions that integrate fully with Bill.com and other third-party applications as necessary.

We incur all technology costs on behalf of our clients, rolling them into our fixed monthly fee. We automate our client invoicing and collections through Bill.com, so money just automatically flows into our bank account. This allows us to focus on what's important: quality work and continued growth.

## What You Will Get Out of Reading this Book

This book not only guides you through getting started with Bill.com, but also addresses how to transition clients, expand your services, and become the most trusted advisor. It will provide you with a thorough knowledge of how Bill.com works, and how it can be customized based on the needs of your firm and the clients you serve.

Also included are tips for selling and pricing your services, along with valuable resources and guidance to help you to easily navigate the setup process. Before you know it, you will be able to use Bill.com to grow your client list and accounting practice.

## Downloadable Files

This book includes supplemental files. Please visit www.sleeter.com/downloads and select this book's title from the drop down menu to download these files.

# Introduction

## Accountants in General

The accounting profession is generally conservative, detail oriented but typically not very creative or adventurous. Long gone are the stereotypical 19th-century accountants, sporting green eyeshades and sleeve protectors, and working by the light of a bankers' lamps, but surprisingly enough there are still large numbers of accountants who use pencil and paper, or spreadsheets and Word documents.

Despite their inability to move beyond their comfort zone, many have continued to grow their firms by adding staff and expanding to multiple locations in an attempt to expand their client base. In keeping with the status quo, they limit their offerings to provide their clients with only traditional services such as tax preparation and planning, which provide a steady, but slowly dwindling, revenue stream.

## *Old World, New World*

In the old world, accountants embraced a business model in which clients managed their own day-to-day finances. Some showed up at year's end with a handwritten check register and a box or receipts, while the more sophisticated ones provided a copy of a data file on removable media such as floppy disks, CDs, or flash drives. It wasn't unusual for these copies to contain broken, inaccurate, or incomplete information that required extensive cleanup before the accountant could prepare financial statements and/or tax returns.

This practice was not only time-consuming and inefficient for firms, but was costly for clients, as it provided them only with a historic summary of how their business performed, as opposed to a snapshot of how it is doing. For many, this was a day late and a dollar short.

The new world enables us to completely rethink and reengineer the services we offer, allowing us to deliver more value and benefit to our clients. Remote access and cloud technologies give us 24/7/365 access to client data, and the ability to be more closely involved with clients' finances throughout the year.

Providing assistance with day-to-day transaction processing, or reviewing data at more frequent intervals, helps to ensure more accurate records and real-time financial reports. Clients of these new world accountants are better prepared to face challenges that may come their way and identify opportunities for growth or improvement.

## The Movement from Servant to Leader

With the coming of Gen Y, the eco-boomers, accountants face increasing demand to offer more value-added services to this rapidly growing segment of business owners. This is creating a social movement, causing the profession to shift from simply reporting on historical events to providing proactive services that include strategic planning, technology consulting, and bookkeeping services.

By joining this movement and embracing collaborative technologies, the role of the accountant will be transformed from one who serves only when called upon to one who leads, one who plays a more important role in the success of this new generation of business owners, earning them the coveted title of "most trusted advisor".

This transformation can also have a positive impact on our Boomer and Gen X clients, as long as they too are willing to join the social movement. For those groups, the change may be more gradual and not without a bit of pain.

The Boomers' and Gen X's motivation for change is different from that of Gen Y; they focus more on transitions and retirement planning. Whether they decide to sell the business or hand it down to the next generation, keeping a pulse on the financial health of the business can have a great impact on the value the business represents for potential buyers or future generations.

For those clients who plant their heels firmly into the ground and refused to join the movement, accounts will have to make the tough decision. Letting them go may be painful, but like ripping off a band aid, but it will hurt only for a moment.

Keeping them on may not hurt now, but will have a significant effect on your ability to transition to the new world and grow.

# Acknowledgements

Writing this book has been a journey, not unlike the one you will embark on to transition your practice to the cloud. Along the way I navigated the startup process, conquered the unknown and overcame fear and a number of obstacles. Trust me when I say the trip was well worth it.

I could not have done this alone so I would like to begin by giving a big shout out to members of The Sleeter Group including Terri Eyden, Charlie Russell, Jeannie Ruesch, Misty Megia, and Tom Sleeter and especially Deborah Pembrook.

Of course, I can't forget Doug Sleeter. Doug, thank you so very much for your trust and patience and for giving me the opportunity to write about something I am so passionate about.

I would also like to thank Rene Lacerte for his vision, leadership, and passion that led to the creation of Bill.com and for allowing me to be a part of something so awesome.

And, finally, to my family, especially my husband Bob who has always believed in me; my dog Gunner who sits patiently in my office each day waiting for me to take a break to throw his red ball; and to Lucky my kitty cat who challenges me daily by napping on my keyboard.

# Chapter 1
# What is Bill.com?

## Overview

Bill.com: the name doesn't even come close to saying it all, as you will learn from this book. This is more than just an awesome, cloud-based application that facilitates bill payment. It is a super tool that can be used to manage all functions related to accounts payable (AP) and accounts receivable (AR). It is a must-have for new world accountants and bookkeepers who support small and medium-sized businesses (SMBs) in their day-to-day accounting operations. Bill.com not only handles the basic tasks associated with those functions, but also eliminates the need for touching and shuffling paper and printing checks. The optional approval process and custom user role features, along with the ability to design your own workflow, helps to ensure tight internal controls, and allows accountants to choose how they want to work with their clients.

In addition to AP and AR, Bill.com offers additional features that include cash-flow forecasting and document storage. The cash-flow forecasting tool eliminates the need for Excel spreadsheets, and helps to easily identify potential troubles before they occur. With the document storages feature, users can create their own file folder system, and store an unlimited number of documents.

Because Bill.com is in the cloud, it is accessible from any device that can access the internet. This gives accountants and their clients the flexibility to work from anywhere, allowing for easier collaboration.

### Accounts Payable Simplified

Business bill payment is a process, unlike consumer bill payment, which usually requires only sending a payment. For businesses, the process includes:

- Paper bills

- Approvals
- Data entry
- Payments
- Document filing/storage

Before Bill.com, the process, as shown in Figure 1-1, was time consuming and often required the constant shuffling of paper among people within the process.

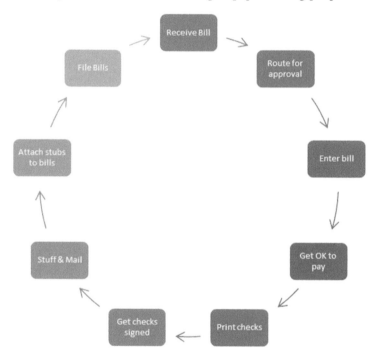

*Figure 1-1 AP Process before Bill.com*

Supporting clients in that process required either on-site services, transfer of information by couriers, or client drop-off and pick-up. To process the work in our office, we needed access to the client's accounting data. If it wasn't cloud-based or hosted on a remote server, it would require transfer of file copies by file share or removable media. The process was also challenging for clients, because they would not have the use of their accounting system until the updated file was returned to them. Failure to properly restore the file could result in data loss, which created more work for both client and accountant.

Bill.com has revolutionized the way we support the process, as shown in Figure 1-2. With the ability to electronically send, share, and store documents, we have eliminated the need to touch paper. After you enter bills into the system, Bill.com automatically sends email notification to the assigned approvers. The email contains a link for the user to login, and automatically redirects them to the page where they can review and approve the bills. During the review process, approvers have the ability to add notes and include additional approvers (based on user permissions). Approvers can deny incorrectly entered bills and bills that require further research. On denial, bills automatically return to the clerk for appropriate action.

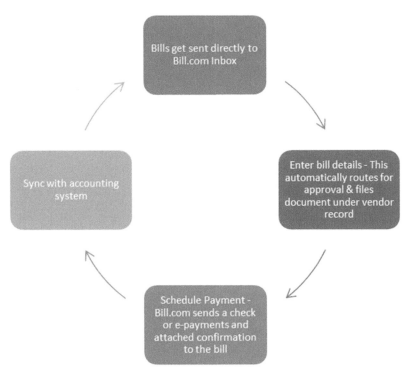

*Figure 1-2 AP Process with Bill.com*

By using the Bill.com payment feature, we no longer need to print and mail checks. We schedule payments to be sent on a chosen date and via desired chosen delivery method: Bill.com e-payment or check. Once the bill payment process is complete, all documents, transaction details, and payment confirmations (including cleared check images) can be accessed by authorized users at any time by any internet-connected device.

Integration with the accounting system eliminates the need for duplicate data entry. Both systems keep all vendor details up to date. Bills sync to the accounting system with all transaction details and payment information stays with the bill.

## Accounts Receivable Simplified

Like AP, managing AR is also a process for SMBs, requiring multiple steps that include:

- Invoice creation
- Customer inquiries
- Collection calls
- Payments
- Document filing/storage

Before Bill.com, the process, as shown in Figure 1-3, was frustrating, difficult to track, and could cause seriously cash-flow issues if not properly managed.

*Figure 1-3 Old AR Process*

Because managing the AR process on behalf of client is a formidable and time-consuming task, many accountants and bookkeepers shy away from offering service for this process. Those of us who dared to take on this task faced many challenges.

Like AP, AR also required access to the client's accounting data and the detailed information necessary to create customer invoices on the client's behalf. Customers usually made inquiries directly to the client, without communicating to the accountant. This often caused additional confusion.

Managing collections on the client's behalf was also time consuming. We would send statements on a regular basis, but refrained from making collection calls on the client's behalf. When clients received payments, they would often deposit them in the bank, but fail to apply them to the invoices, creating a mess in AR, overstating income, and requiring a lot of cleanup work.

Figure 1-4 shows how Bill.com has simplified the way we manage AR, not only for our clients but for our practice as well. You can create one-time or recurring invoices and send them via email or snail mail. Customers have a portal where they can set up one-time or automatic payments from their checking, PayPal, or credit card account.

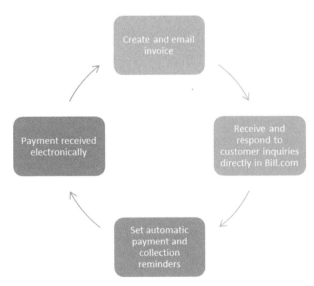

*Figure 1-4 AR Process with Bill.com*

The portal also gives customers the ability to view previously sent invoices and supporting documents. When customers need additional information regarding invoices, they can post comments that the system then emails to the invoice sender. These comments and responses are date and time stamped, and retained in the account for future reference.

To eliminate the sending of statements, you can customize three levels of automatic email reminders to accommodate your messages and schedules, and the system sends them from the client's email address. This feature also allows reminders to be sent in advance of the payment due date, greatly reducing the potential of overdue payments.

## Cash Forecasting

Cash is king. This is especially true for our SMB clients or early-stage start-ups. Since most do not have a crystal ball at their disposal, they have the challenge of finding alternative methods for projecting cash flows. Excel spreadsheets have been the primary go-to application for most SMBs and accountants; but that method requires repeated manual updating to ensure accurate projections. Those who lack the skills or time necessary to manage those tasks often resort to primitive methods, such as pencil and paper, or forego this critical task altogether.

The Bill.com cash-flow forecasting tool makes it easy for accountants to help their clients better understand their projected inflows, outflows, and cash balances out to three months. Cash flows are projected using the bank account balance (synchronized from the accounting system or manually entered), and transactions already entered for AP and AR. Because you do not enter all transactions as AP or AR, this feature allows for input of non-Bill.com transactions such as:

- Daily cash sales
- Payroll
- Automatic debits and/or credits

This feature provides three viewing options, allowing users to select the format that works best for them. These options are:

- Visual graph (Figure 1-5)

- Calendar view (Figure 1-6)
- List view

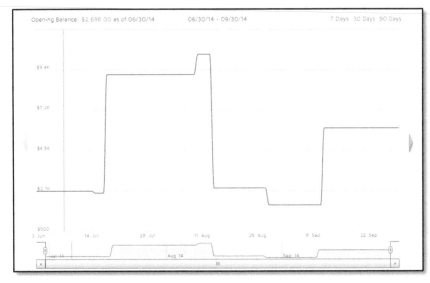

*Figure 1-5 Bill.com cash flow graph*

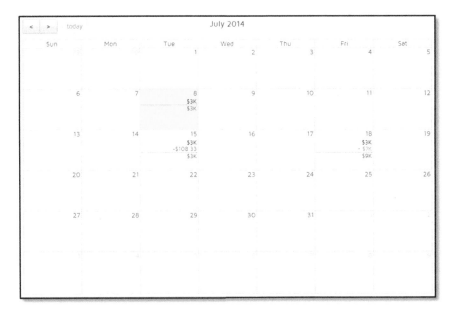

*Figure 1-6 Bill.com cash flow calendar*

All forecast views are interactive, allowing users to make changes to transactions on the fly. These changes include scheduling a bill payment, editing the date of an existing bill payment, or updating the date on which you expect the customer payments to arrive.

## Document Storage

Like it or not, document retention and storage is one of the necessary evils of owning a business. For those clients who have not yet embraced digital storage, this can be an expensive and frustrating process. Not only are they incurring the cost of folders, bankers' boxes, and offsite storage, they also are paying someone to (hopefully) file everything in the right place. If they need information while away from the office, they must rely on others to retrieve and send a copy, or provide them with the pertinent details.

For clients who are using Bill.com, the transition to digital storage can be much more seamless, since they are already storing bills and invoices within a system they trust and feel comfortable with. Each Bill.com account includes unlimited document storage with the ability to create a custom file folder system to meet each client's individual needs. In addition to filing in folders, you can also tag or cross-file documents by attaching them to the following categories:

- Bills
- Vendors
- Customers
- Invoices
- Invoice payments
- Accounts

Because the documents are stored as digital images, no one can edit them, eliminating to potential for manipulation. You can, however, open Microsoft Word or Excel documents uploaded or emailed to the inbox in their original format, but changes cannot be saved to the original digitally filed copy.

## Accounting System Integration

To eliminate the need for duplicate data entry and the concomitant potential for error, integration is one of the key factors I consider when looking at applications for streamlining operations. There are lots of applications on the market that claim to integrate well, but many do not provide the level of detail we require.

Bill.com provides a seamless and deep integration with the most popular accounting systems used by accountants and SMBs today, including:

- QuickBooks for Windows (all versions)
- QuickBooks online (Essentials and Plus)
- Intacct
- NetSuite
- Xero

Using either native or third-party sync applications, depending on which accounting system you use, Bill.com syncs information automatically or by the simple click of a button. These sync applications import information into the accounting system with the same level detail as if you had entered it directly. Security settings within the sync applications eliminate the potential for missing or duplicated data. In the event problems do occur during the sync process, the application notifies the user and suggests fixes to resolve the issue.

The flow of information to and from Bill.com differs in relation to the accounting software you're using. All integrations transfer bill and bill payment information into the accounting software, but only a few allow for two-way data transfer. In most instances, the chart of accounts and customer and vendor lists flow in both directions, allowing users to add or update in either one. AR integration is also available, but it too is specific to the accounting software with which it is integrating. Figure 1-7 is an example of how information flows between Bill.com and QuickBooks desktop for Windows. We will get into more detail about integration later on.

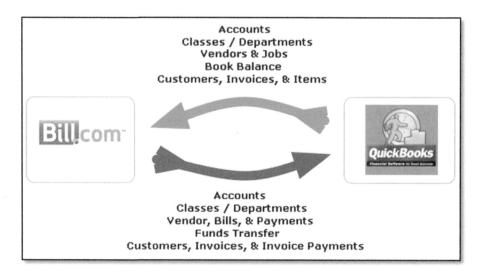

*Figure 1-7 Bill.com sync with QuickBooks for Windows*

## Summary

So as you can see, Bill.com is more than just an online bill payment system. With its robust features and seamless integration, accountants can support clients at almost any level, from bill entry to full-service AP and AR management. Features such as custom user roles and approval policies support a clear separation of duties and tight internal controls. And with the added features of cash-flow forecasting, document storage, and mobile access, Bill.com can help to grow your practice by offering more value-added services to clients.

# Chapter 2
# What Problems Does It Solve?

## What Problems?

We often don't realize that problems exist until an incident occurs that brings them to light. The effect of such problems, if not resolved properly, can result in irreparable damage to the accountant-client relationship or the firm's reputation. Our typical response was to take the necessary action, put out the fire, and repair the damage as best we could. Once the situation was under control, we could go back to business as usual and maybe not take time to explore the cause and contrive a long-term solution.

Many problems are the result of inefficient and poorly designed manual processes. Such manual processes often lack contingency plans for interrupted workflow, or internal controls that safeguard the security of clients' data.

## Problem 1: Paper Exchange

As we all know, documents are a necessary part of offering client accounting services. What we may not realize, however, is how expensive, time-consuming, and inconvenient the exchange of paper can be. In this section, I will address the most common methods of exchange, the problems they can cause, and how Bill.com can solve them.

## *Client Drop-off and Pick-up*

Sure this sound like an easy solution, mainly because the client is doing all the work, but have you ever thought about the impact it can have on office productivity?

Many clients perceive a deviation from their daily routine as a welcome break. A visit to the accountants' office gives them an opportunity to socialize. Interruptions like these, however, not only take up valuable time but can cause distractions in workflow, increasing the chance of errors. Clients may also consider these visits an opportune time to solicit free advice not related to the work at hand.

Conversely, the constant rise in gas prices may drive some clients away from stopping by to drop off or pick up documents. Other clients may perceive taking time out of their already busy schedules as an expensive yet necessary inconvenience. Eventually, other firms may sway these clients by the offer of a more convenient and economical way to transfer documents.

## *Courier Services (FedEx, UPS, USPS)*

This method reduces interruptions and eliminates the demands on customer time, but it can be both expensive and unreliable. Standard next-day courier fees for one-way local delivery range from $18 to $27 each way for an envelope weighing less than one pound. Absorbing even a portion of those fees can negatively affect a firm's profitability. Yet passing the fees on to the clients as billable items increases the client's cost and may leave them feeling nickeled and dimed.

As reliable as those carriers claim to be, delays are not uncommon and can result in work bottlenecks for your office staff. The trickle-down effect of such delays may result in late bill payments on behalf of the client. In addition to delays, packages can get lost altogether. Imagine the amount of work involved in trying to recreate a shipment of lost original documents. The contents of a package that got lost in transit back to the client may be easier to re-create, but will still result in lost time for the firm and/or additional cost for the client.

## *The Solution*

Bill.com offers a convenient solution to these problems that will increase efficiency, reduce cost, and eliminate the potential for documents lost in transit. Every Bill.com account is assigned a dedicated email address and fax number that clients (or their vendors) can use to send the documents directly to their Bill.com inbox, as shown in Figure 2-1. Once received, documents are available for processing at any time. Once processed, bills are neatly organized and filed under the vendor record, and accessible to all users with the appropriate permissions. You can tag all other documents with additional information and store them in folders.

Clients will no longer suffer the inconvenience and cost associated with drop-off and pick-up or courier fees. Additionally, this eliminates office interruptions, reducing the potential for errors and increasing productivity.

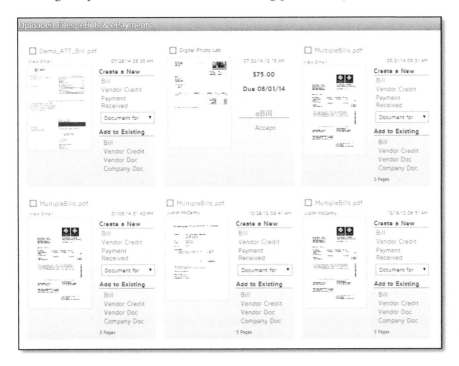

*Figure 2-1 The Bill.com inbox*

## Problem 2: Travel Time and Scope Creep

Like many firms, we spent years providing on-site bookkeeping and payroll services for our SMB clients. We could not have imagined a world in which we could serve them remotely. How would we get all the documents, access to their accounting data, and the approvals we needed to pay bills? We honestly believed that our clients liked having us in their offices, and that they could not survive without seeing our pretty faces on a regular schedule.

Continuing to service clients in this manner was not scalable without adding additional staff. Additionally, travel to client locations while on the clock required us to carry additional liability insurance, further decreasing our profit margins.

We imposed a three-hour minimum to guarantee that the trip would be worth our time. If we completed the assignment early, it was not unusual for the client to assign us other duties, as we were charging them by the hour. These other duties went beyond the terms of the original engagement, and in most cases were services for which we may have billed a higher rate.

### The Solution

Bill.com helped us solve these problems, and allowed us to grow while reducing our overhead. It gave us the ability to receive documents, process AP and AR, and schedule payments from anywhere. Connected to a cloud-based or a hosted accounting system, it eliminated the need for onsite services and the associated travel time.

This also allowed us to migrate to a fixed-fee, value-billing structure. We charge our clients for the value of the service we provide, not for the time it takes us to do it. When a client requested additional services, they were billed the appropriate rate. This eliminated scope creep and increased our profit margins.

Our clients, much as they liked seeing us, found our new service model to be more convenient. No longer must they remain in their office on our scheduled day, or relinquish a desk and computer for the duration of the appointment, making it a win-win situation.

## Problem 3: Internal Fraud

Of all the problems that accountants and SMBs face, fraud is the most serious. In addition to the adverse effect it can have on our clients' business, if a member of the firm is involved, it is likely to have significant impact on the reputation and longevity of the accounting practice. For that reason, I am pulling out the big guns here: Look at these staggering statistics.

According to a 2014 study conducted by the Association of Certified Fraud Examiners (ACFE), nearly 24 percent of companies with fewer than one hundred employees are victims of fraud, resulting in a median loss of $145,000. As shown in Figure 2-2, 28 percent of these incidents related to billing schemes while 22 percent involved check tampering.

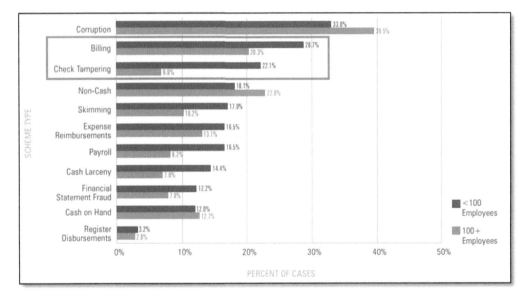

*Figure 2-2 Percent of fraud by scheme type*

Other important findings of this study were as follows:

- A typical organization loses five percent of revenue each year to fraud.
- Nearly half of all fraudulent acts were perpetrated by workers in the accounting, operations, or sales departments.

- One-third of those cases lacked appropriate internal controls to prevent the fraud.
- Lack of internal controls was the primary weakness in more than 41 percent of cases at organizations with fewer than one hundred employees.

Over the past few years, we have seen a significant number of fraud cases involving accounting firms. For many, this is due to not holding business owners accountable for making financial decisions. Firms that cater to or accommodate their SMB clients are especially at risk. Without proper controls, staff can take advantage of the following situations:

- Improper storage and control over check stock
- Staff ability to alter or destroy original documents
- Permission to pay bills without client or supervisor approvals
- Lack of audit trails and/or failure to document approvals
- Access to customer payments and the ability to alter or delete invoices

## Solution

Bill.com is a cost-effective way to greatly reduce or eliminate the potential for internal fraud. The system includes features that make it easy to implement internal controls and define a clear separation of duties. Mobile access makes it easier for accountants to require client involvement in decision making. Here is a list of the Bill.com features that prevent fraud, and how they help to eliminate it.

- *User Roles* – Determines a user's level of permissions. Included is a permission that limits the ability to pay only bills that have been approved
- *Approvals* – Set preferences that do not allow changes to be made to bills that have already been approved
- *Approval Policies* – Set approval policies for bills and vendor credits, including threshold amounts, minimum number of approvers, and/or specific approvers
- *Authorized Payers* – Only users with the appropriate permission who have been authorized and verified are able to schedule, cancel, void, or reissue bill payments

- *Audit Trail* – Tracks changes to transactions by timestamp and user name. Indicates which fields were changed, and includes both old and new values
- *Payments (AP)* – Eliminates the need for stored check stock and signature stamps. Once check payments are cleared, an image of the check is attached to the payment summary
- *Payments (AR)* – Allows customers to pay electronically, eliminating payment theft

With the proper set up, these features help to clearly define a workflow and separation of duties. This will not only protect your clients, but also reduces the liability of the accounting firm.

# Problem 4: External Fraud

Even when implementing tight internal controls, we are still vulnerable to the threat of external fraud. Every time you send a paper check to a vendor, the following account information is available to anyone who has access to it:

- Company name
- Company address
- ABA routing number
- Account number
- Account owner's signature

Anyone can buy blank check stock and MICR toner online or at office supply stores. While many retailers will ship these products only to the credit card billing address, there are still plenty that will ship anywhere. These supplies, along with check printing software that requires no internet connection or account verification, enables malefactors to create checks drawn on your account. This fraudulent activity can easily go undetected if account owners do not regularly monitor their bank account activity.

Some of the larger banks offer Positive Pay fraud protection, a service that requires account owners to upload a register file to their bank every night. The system matches checks presented against the account to the file, and sends exception alerts to the account owner to review and approve or deny. While this seems like a great solution, in most cases it is prohibitively expensive for small business owners.

## Solution

Business owners can protect their bank account information by utilizing the Bill.com bill pay feature. The system sends all payments made via Bill.com to vendors as electronic payments or checks drawn on Bill.com's bank account. This eliminates public exposure of your account information, and thereby greatly reduces the potential for fraud.

# Problem 5: Document Storage and Access

I recently took on a new client, and while reviewing her financials found a monthly expense of $159 for rental of storage space. When I inquired what she kept in her storage unit, she explained that is was her archived paper files from previous years. This client, like many, does not have enough office space to store this information, which the IRS and the state department of revenue require.

In addition to the expense of storage, there also is the challenge of retrieval. Because the closest storage facility is on the other side of town, getting access to historical documents is disruptive and time consuming.

Even for clients who have space to accommodate on-site storage, there are challenges. Mobile staff are at the mercy of office staff to convey information contained in a filed document when they are away from the office. Paper can easily be misfiled, lost, or destroyed, making the process of retrieval difficult or even impossible.

## Solution

As discussed earlier in this chapter, Bill.com provides a convenient way to convert documents to digital images by sending them to the Bill.com inbox. From there, you can link them to transactions, tag them, and/or file them in folders. Because you cannot alter document images, auditors accept them, allowing for the shredding or destruction of originals.

If a client chooses to cancel the Bill.com account, that client can purchase a DVD that contains images of all processed documents for a nominal fee. Active account owners can also request a DVD for a specific period of time, which may be helpful for audit purposes. In addition to the images of processed documents, the DVD contains images of cleared bill-payment checks sent via Bill.com, as shown in Figure 2-3.

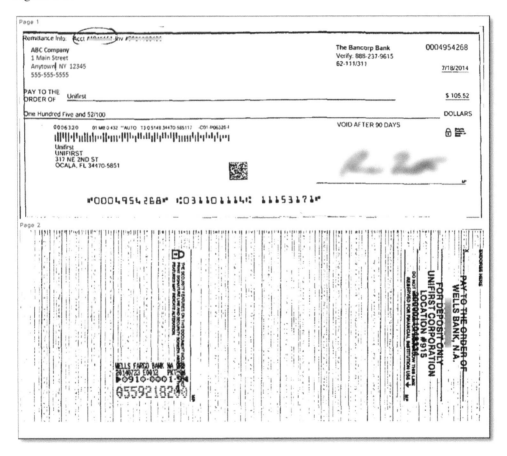

*Figure 2-3 Cleared Check Image*

## Summary

As you can see, some of the most basic processes contain problems waiting to happen. By taking a proactive approach and implementing new procedures, you can eliminate those problems before they have a negative effect on your practice or client relationships.

Setting up approval policies and user permission will help establish tight internal controls and create a clear separation of duties. This, and the ability to pay and be paid via Bill.com, contribute to increased levels of security, protecting all parties involved.

Using Bill.cm to receive, store, and share documents saves clients the cost and hassle of drop-offs and/or couriers. It also helps to establish the groundwork for migrating from on-site to remote services, providing accounting firms the freedom to grow their practices while delivering added value to their clients.

# Chapter 3
# How Does It Fit into Your Accounting Practice?

## Growing Your Practice, Delivering More Value

According to Henry Ford, "If you always do what you've always done, you will always get what you always got." Accountants looking to grow their practices must embrace change, and adopt new technologies in order to stay competitive. Software applications such as Bill.com can help increase productivity without the need to add staff or grow the brick-and-mortar infrastructure. Embracing these changes allows firms to deliver a higher level of service, which will lead to greater client retention, more quality referrals, and other new clients.

Over the past several years, I have had the pleasure of helping hundreds of accountants and bookkeepers grow or transform their practices by implementing Bill.com. The majority were amazed at the impact the adoption of a single application could have on their ability to support clients in their day-to-day operations.

For accountants who already offer ongoing client accounting services, Bill.com increases their efficiency, allowing them to serve more clients and deliver more value simultaneously. For those looking to migrate away from providing monthly write-up, adopting Bill.com can transform their service away from compiling after-the-fact reports, to working with clients collaboratively. Books stay up to date throughout the month.

Accountants looking to expand their practices by adding a new line of service find Bill.com to be an integral part of the process. It allows them to develop interactive processes, and provides their staff with a seamless way to work collaboratively with clients.

## Transforming Existing Bookkeeping Services

Bill.com is the perfect solution for accountants and bookkeepers looking to transform their existing services. It eliminates the hassle of exchanging documents and because it is cloud based you can access it from any device connected to the internet. This allows staff the flexibility to work from home when they are unable to make it into the office due to bad weather or child care issues. It also expands the reach of the firm, providing the opportunity to not only hire talent from outside their local area, but expand their reach for clients.

Developing an AP workflow that includes multiple people, each with a unique permissions profile, can create a digital assembly-line effect. Entry-level staff or Bill.com's data-entry service can handle basic data entry. Senior staff can use the approval process to review the entries, editing as necessary. This reduces the demand on their time, allowing them to focus on higher-value services. Adding the client as a second approver in the process keeps them engaged.

Scheduling payments via Bill.com increases efficiency even more by eliminating the need to print checks and the tasks associated with that. It also reduces the number of individual payment transactions on the bank statement, simplifying reconciliation.

Figure 3-1 illustrates how much more efficient the AP process can be when using Bill.com.

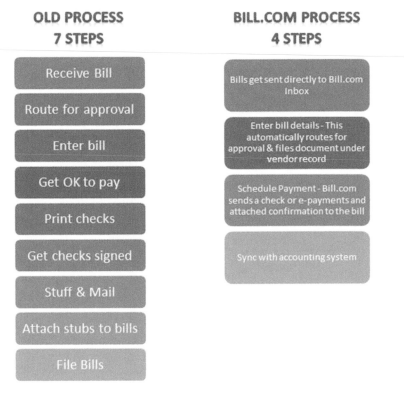

*Figure 3-1 Old AP process vs. Bill.com process*

The AR feature in Bill.com enables working collaboratively with your clients, such as in managing invoices and collections. Clients can create invoices directly in Bill.com while in the office or on the road. Leaving invoices in the send queue provides an opportunity for office or accounting staff to review and edit prior to sending. When your clients receive payments electronically, Bill.com automatically applies them to the proper invoices. This reduces guesswork when you do not have all the details for posting deposits into the accounting system.

Setting up Bill.com to automatically send email reminders for overdue invoices reduces uncollected receivables, and make the accountant look like a superhero.

Figure 3-2 illustrates how much more efficient the AR process can be when using Bill.com.

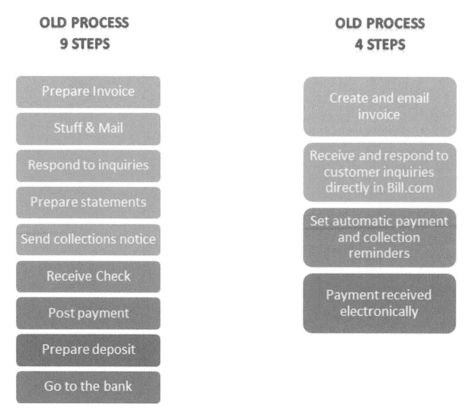

**OLD PROCESS
9 STEPS**

Prepare Invoice

Stuff & Mail

Respond to inquiries

Prepare statements

Send collections notice

Receive Check

Post payment

Prepare deposit

Go to the bank

**OLD PROCESS
4 STEPS**

Create and email invoice

Receive and respond to customer inquiries directly in Bill.com

Set automatic payment and collection reminders

Payment received electronically

*Figure 3-2 Old AR process vs. Bill.com process*

## Expanding Client Services

When I learned accounting in the early 1980s, we used pencil and paper journals and ledgers. At month's end, the business owner would submit these to their accountants for review. The accountant would then make adjustments in handwritten entries, and compile the financial reports. That is what we referred to as client write-up work.

Fast forward to today. Single-entry accounting software has replaced pencil and paper journals. These systems compile the information into user-generated reports. Add cloud access and hosted data to this, and reactive client services such as write-up soon become a thing of the past.

The impending extinction of that level of service opens the door for traditional accounting firms to venture into the new world of client accounting services. In this new world, accountants play a proactive role in the day-to-day operations of their clients' businesses, helping them to maintain order and manage their financial operations in real time.

Implementing Bill.com provides an opportunity to expand services that deliver added value and benefits. Clients can handle the daily tasks of entering and paying bills via Bill.com, assigning the accountant as an approver. This shared platform provides the accountant instant access to review the account, class, or item categorization. It also reduces the need for manual entries to make corrections at month's end.

Setting clients up to use the AR features empowers them to better manage collections, giving them more control over their cash flow. By encouraging them to request electronic payments from their customers, you help to ensure the correct application of each payment to its invoice. This also reduces the need for end-of-month corrections.

Managing client work throughout the month frees accountants from peaks and valleys in their work load throughout the month. More real-time access to accurate and up-to-date reports helps clients manage their businesses better and make better financial decisions. Clients will recognize the added value, and have a deeper appreciation for the accountant's work.

## Adding New Service Lines

To stay competitive in today's market, traditional CPA firms are looking to expand their scope of services beyond tax planning and preparation. By adding client accounting to their menu of services, they are more likely to attract new clients. Introducing these services to existing clients provides an opportunity for deeper engagement and a closer relationship.

By implementing Bill.com internally, firms are able to expand into new markets, providing assistance in the following areas:

Accounts payable

- Entering bills to ensure proper account classification
- Scheduling just-on-time payments to better manage cash flow
- Filing and storing bills digitally
- Managing vendor payment inquiries

Accounts receivable

- Creating and sending customer invoices
- Managing the reminder and collections process
- Receiving payments electronically
- Managing customer account inquiries
- Filing and storing invoices and supporting documents digitally

Document storage (in addition to bills and invoices)

- Bank statements
- Financial reports
- Contracts
- Price lists
- Payroll reports and quarterly forms
- Employee records

Cash-flow forecasting (out to three months)

- Using your book balance for your primary bank account
- Automatically subtracting bills scheduled for payment
- Automatically adding payments scheduled for receipt
- Ability to add non-Bill.com activity in the projections

For clients who already manage their own accounting, recommending Bill.com presents an opportunity to work collaboratively. Sharing responsibilities allows clients to retain control over cash flow without the hassle of entering bills and creating invoices. It also provides them the freedom to access this information using the Bill.com mobile app. As shown in Figure 3-3, this allows clients to:

- Approve bills
- Schedule bill payments
- View open customer invoices and aging

- View received and scheduled customer payments

*Figure 3-3 Bill.com mobile app*

Whether you provide full or assisted service, being more closely involved in clients' day-to-day operations gives accountants better insight. This enables them to offer more proactive tax planning advice throughout the year, and reduces the time required to prepare tax returns. Delivering added benefits and value to customers helps to increase client retention and leads to more referral business.

## Summary

As you can see, Bill.com is the perfect tool for accounting firms looking to build, expand or transform their practice. It can also be a vital part of the equation for those that are just starting out.

Changing how you process work internally increases productivity and reduces errors. Moving from "after-the-fact" to "in-the-now services" delivers added value to clients and frees up firm resources providing opportunities for growth.

# Chapter 4
# Overcoming Obstacles

## Encountering Obstacles

Change is never easy, especially for the accounting world. When implementing new technologies such as Bill.com, it is common to encounter obstacles along the way. For some, the effort to avoid such obstacles seems to make the process even more difficult, and appears to justify abandoning the project. So it's important to keep your eye on the prize, and remember the great benefits you will enjoy by transitioning to Bill.com.

- Growth and increased profits
- Process standardization
- Tighter controls
- Efficiency
- Happy clients
- Happy employees
- Less stress
- Mobility
- Better client retention
- Better work-life balance

To ensure a seamless transition, you will first need to identify the particular types of obstacles your firm may face. While each practice will face a different set of obstacles, some of the most common are as follows:

- Fear of change and/or staff resistance
- Fear of the cloud
- Client resistance

Once you have identified what challenges you may face, you will be better prepared to develop a plan to address and overcome them.

## Fear of Change

A few years ago, I was working with an accounting firm that was thinking about implementing Bill.com to increase internal efficiency and support clients outside the local area better. During the initial discussions, one of the partners objected to the changes, stating that they would be difficult and could create internal havoc. He indicated that his staff did not adapt well to change, and that implementing a new process would be disruptive to their operations. When I asked what his staff's biggest fears and concerns were, however, he was unable to name any.

I suggested that we set up a meeting with members of the staff to introduce them to Bill.com, giving them an opportunity to ask questions and present their concerns. As the meeting progressed I wasn't surprised; I had heard most of these same concerns many times before. What it really boiled down to was that they feared change. And it wasn't just the staff who felt that way; the partner that originally voiced the objection admitted he had many of the same concerns himself.

For this team it wasn't fear of the results of change, it was fear of the process. Apparently, they had been through some mishandled instances of change, and so created a stressful environment.

Here are some of the concerns expressed at that meeting and how we addressed them.

### We Don't Have Time to Learn Something New

There was ample time within their schedules to attend training. The real issue was that, in the past they had not had structured training or the opportunity to practice the new systems before those systems went live.

We developed a plan to provide the staff with structured hands-on training and access to a demo company so that they could practice what they had learned. We also introduced them to the Bill.com in-product videos, which you can use as a refresher or reference.

Providing staff with available time and access to training gives them the knowledge and confidence they need to feel comfortable. Of course, it will also help to ensure that they will use the system properly, reducing stress and the potential for problems.

## How Will We Get Support When We Run into Problems?

This concern wasn't really with how they would get support; it was more about the level of service they would receive. Long hold times and frustrating interactions with other software companies made them wonder if the same would be true when they needed help with Bill.com.

During the training, the instructor showed the team how to access the Bill.com support site, as shown in Figure 4-1. He demonstrated how quick and easy it was to engage with a support agent by chat or by requesting a callback. He also showed them how they could search the knowledge base and the Bill.com community for answers.

Bill.com provides U.S.-based support to all users for free. Wait times for chat support, which is the most popular channel, are minimal, usually less than one minute. Most inquiries can be resolved with a single support session. Those that require additional research are escalated quickly, and can be easily tracked from your support history file in the Bill.com support center.

*Figure 4-1 Bill.com support page*

## *It Will Take More Time*

What this really meant was that they didn't trust the integration. For this reason, they felt the need to manually verify that all transactions were posted properly to the accounting system. This concern stemmed from past issues with other applications that did not do a very good job integrating, or that imported only summary journal entries.

We provided a demonstration and explained how Bill.com integrated with their accounting system. Bill.com imports transactions into the accounting system in the same manner as if someone had entered them directly. We also showed them how Bill.com provides notification when issues do arise, along with possible solutions to resolve them as shown in Figure 4-2. This provided the team with the confidence they needed to no longer manually verify the entries.

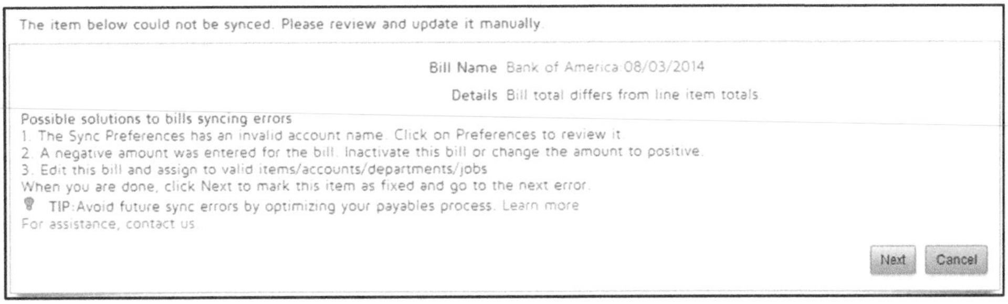

The item below could not be synced. Please review and update it manually.

> Bill Name  Bank of America 08/03/2014
>
> Details  Bill total differs from line item totals.

Possible solutions to bills syncing errors:
1. The Sync Preferences has an invalid account name. Click on Preferences to review it.
2. A negative amount was entered for the bill. Inactivate this bill or change the amount to positive.
3. Edit this bill and assign to valid items/accounts/departments/jobs.
When you are done, click Next to mark this item as fixed and go to the next error.
💡 TIP: Avoid future sync errors by optimizing your payables process. Learn more
For assistance, contact us.

[ Next ]  [ Cancel ]

*Figure 4-2 Solutions to resolve a sync error*

## It Won't Work for My Clients

If I had a dollar for every time I heard that, I wouldn't be writing this book. I'd be sitting on a tropical beach, sipping margaritas. We must dissect this subject to understand what the staff member was actually trying to say. It may be that there were special circumstances regarding how work was performed for specific clients. Maybe they used purchase orders or tracked inventory. It could also have been referring to clients who were technically challenged and didn't adapt well to change themselves.

In this particular case, I asked the staff member to give me an example of why she felt Bill.com would not work for her clients. None of her reasons had anything to do with the technical aspects of Bill.com or the abilities of her clients. It was more about the way she managed the process and she couldn't understand how Bill.com would work with it.

In most cases, transitioning to Bill.com will require a change in process and procedures. The good news, however, is that the transition will help develop a more seamless workflow, creating efficiencies for clients and the accounting staff alike.

## We Don't Know How to Get Started

This is a valid concern, and one that we will address. Getting started with something new is always a challenge, but preparation will make getting started easier. Consider what information you need to gather, and develop a workflow in advance. That will help you to easily navigate the set-up process.

When you first log into a new Bill.com account, you have the option to go to the Startup Checklist, as shown in Figure 4-3. This page will navigate you through the basic set up so that you can begin using Bill.com.

Chapter 6 will provide you with a full overview of how Bill.com works and what information you will need to prepare to ensure a seamless set up. In Chapter 7, I will walk you through the account setup so you can begin using Bill.com quickly.

*Figure 4-3 Bill.com Startup Checklist*

# Suspicion Concerning Cloud Security

In a recent meeting with a local small business owner, I suggested using Bill.com as a way to reduce the time he spent creating invoices and paying bills. He responded by telling me he would prefer to keep his data on his local computer because he feels it's safer than being in the cloud.

Concerns about security are one of the top excuses that organizations use for not adopting cloud services. The biggest fear is compromised accounting data and banking information. The other major concern is the potential for data to be lost irretrievably.

Bill.com, like today's most popular cloud-based accounting solutions, is committed to protecting the security and privacy of your information. It provides best-in-class security, which includes firewalls to prevent unauthorized electronic access, and SSL encryption technology that ensures the privacy of communications between your browser and the Bill.com service.

The servers run in a high-security facility with biometric access controls. This prevents unauthorized physical access. To eliminate the potential for loss, Bill.com continuously backs up all data off-site, so in the event of a disaster Bill.com is able to quickly recover all data.

For small businesses that store their accounting data on their local computer or server, the security risks are far greater. Consumer-grade Internet security applications and firewalls cannot protect local data from dedicated hackers.

In the event of disaster or hard drive failure, data can be lost completely. For those who are diligent about backing up their data, recovery may be much easier. But if you had backed up on removable media and stored the data at the same location, they will most likely suffer the same fate as the computer hard drive.

Sensitive information such as bank account and credit card numbers are also at risk if stored locally. In the event of a break-in or unauthorized physical access, this information could fall into the hands of potential fraudsters. If not detected quickly, fraudulent activity is likely to occur and could result in a financial loss.

By going over this information with the small business owner, I was able to eliminate his fears, eventually get his business set up on Bill.com, and convince him to adopt a cloud-based accounting system to manage his business finances.

## Client Resistance

When clients are resistant to change, it creates an uneasy feeling and fear that they may go elsewhere for their accounting services. Ironically, moving to a new accountant would be a much bigger adjustment than the adoption of a new process, so it's more than likely your clients will stay with you and learn to adapt. If they do elect to go elsewhere, there were probably other factors involved in their decision.

To overcome client resistance, it is best to start by listening to them and understanding what their objections are. It's likely they will have many of the same concerns that have already gone over. Because you have already addressed those concerns, you will be better prepared to put the client's mind at ease. Some other typical concerns are:

- Will there be additional charges?
- Will I have less control?
- What happens if I decide to leave the firm or Bill.com?
- Will I need to upgrade my hardware?

Full-service accounting firms that have already adopted a fixed-fee billing model may choose to absorb the cost of Bill.com service. This is because using Bill.com internally helps to increase efficiency, reduce the cost of delivery, and grow profit margins. For those who are still billing for time and costs, this change in service provides an opportunity to adopt a fixed-fee billing structure. Bill.com strongly encourages this billing model, and provides resources to help you price your services effectively.

For those who elect to bill their clients directly, it's important to clearly explain the benefits and value that Bill.com delivers. In addition to the security features and time savings, it can also eliminate the need to purchase preprinted invoice forms, check stock, postage, and envelopes.

You can ease a client's fear of losing control by educating them on how the process works. Explaining how user permissions and a clearly defined workflow offers better control provides them with a clear understanding and sense of security.

If the time comes that your client decides to leave the firm or bring their accounting in house, they can still access their Bill.com account. To ensure a seamless transition, accountants are encouraged to address the specifics within the client's engagement letter or service contract. Users with the role of administrator can remove client accounts from the accountant's console. If the account does not transition to another accountant's console, Bill.com will consider it a retail subscription and bill it at a higher rate.

If the client elects to leave Bill.com altogether, they have the option to purchase a DVD that contains all their document images, as covered in Chapter 2. Bill.com also gives its customers the option to access their data for up to three years.

Finally, there is also no need to worry about upgrading hardware. Bill.com is a web-based application that you can access through your favorite internet browser. To ensure the best experience and access to all features Bill.com recommends keeping your browser up to date with the latest version.

## Summary

According to the late American screenwriter Frank Howard Clark, if you find a path with no obstacles, it probably doesn't lead anywhere. As you start down the path to implementing Bill.com, you will most certainly face obstacles. By anticipating these obstacles, you will be better prepared to overcome them.

As you continue down the path, navigation will become much easier and you will soon arrive to your destination, the new world of client accounting services.

# Chapter 5
# How to Help Your Clients

## Don't Sell, Be a Problem Solver

One of the most common questions I hear when I talk to accountants about Bill.com is, "How do I sell it?" For those of us in the accounting professions, the thought of trying to get our clients to try something new can be terrifying. One of the biggest reasons for this fear is that we are concerned about how our clients will perceive us.

Think about how you feel when a telemarketer calls, trying to sell you a new home security system. Do you feel that they are really concerned about your security, or are just trying to make a buck? And what if you already have a home security system, doesn't it anger you that they interrupted your dinner to sell you something that you don't need?

We don't want our clients to think that we are just trying to get more of their money by selling them something that that already have, such as a way to pay bills and invoice customers. This is especially true if you were the one who set them up with their current solution.

So the secret to selling Bill.com is... *don't!* Yes, you heard right, don't sell Bill.com to your clients. Instead, position yourself as a problem solver, because after all, that really is what you are. By expressing your real interest in your clients and how their processes do or don't work, you will have a more advantageous position when the time comes to present a solution.

## Figure Out Where it hurts

So, how do you figure out what their problems or pain points are? If you ask them directly, they will either tell you they don't have any problems or the floodgates will open. Either way, when the conversation ends, you probably won't have the answers you were looking for.

To help you become a better problem solver, here are a few ideas for diagnosing client pain as a step toward getting them on board with Bill.com.

## Lunch and Listen

Who doesn't love a free meal? Bringing lunch to your client's office is a terrific way to get them and their staff to talk with you candidly. But to do this effectively, you will want to follow these guidelines:

### Include the "Why" in the Invitation

You want to be sure that your clients know why you are calling these meetings, so they can share the conversation with their staff to help them be better prepared. You may want to say that you are researching some new technologies. During the lunch meeting, explain that their input and feedback will help prepare you for your upcoming meetings with vendors.

By using this approach, your clients and their staff will feel invested in your decision making. So when the time comes to introduce them to Bill.com, they will be more likely to listen with an open mind.

### Keep it Short

Limit the meeting to 60 minutes. Remember, their time is valuable too, and you don't want to be a distraction or a drag on their productivity.

### Who Should Attend?

If your client runs a small organization, you should consider including the whole team so that no one feels left out. For larger organizations you should be specific, including only those who deal directly with AP and AR.

### Keep it Simple

You don't need to plan an elaborate spread. My suggestion is to order a platter of assorted sandwiches from my local deli, along with bags of chips, canned soft drinks, and a plate of assorted cookies. Be sure to ask if there are any vegetarians or any with other dietary needs in the group; you don't want anyone to feel left out. And don't forget to bring plates, utensils, cups, and napkins.

### Prepare Professionally

Arrive 15 minutes early, so that you can prepare the meeting space. This will speed the process when the lunch begins, and allow you to devote more time to the conversation. Take responsibility for cleaning up at the end.

Prepare some probing questions that will move the conversation in the right direction. They may be something like:

- What is the most painful part of managing AP?
- If you could eliminate one step of the process, what would it be, and why?
- Do you feel there are weaknesses in the process, and if so, what are they?
- What is the most painful part of managing AR?
- If you could eliminate one step of the process, what would it be, and why?
- How do you manage the collection process for overdue invoices?

You may also want to request permission to record the meeting. This will eliminate your need to take notes.

## Observe Their Current Process

Observing how your clients and/or their staff manage the AP and AR processes will give you insight into their areas of weakness and/or inefficiency. This can also provide an opportunity to interact with them on an individual basis, and give them an opportunity to open up and share their ideas and struggles.

The tricky part of this method is in finding takers. Clients may feel a bit uneasy if you present this offer to them directly, so consider sending out a general email to a small sampling of clients. In that email, offer a limited number of evaluations and set an expiration date. That way, you will create an urgent call to action that will get the ball rolling.

Whether you choose to offer this service at no charge or for a nominal fee, you will want to provide a simple report of your findings followed by a scheduled visit to review and offer solutions.

Figure 5-1 provides an example of how you may present your finding and recommendations to the client.

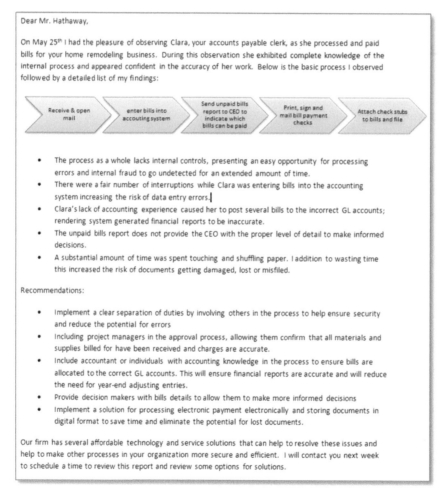

Dear Mr. Hathaway,

On May 25th I had the pleasure of observing Clara, your accounts payable clerk, as she processed and paid bills for your home remodeling business. During this observation she exhibited complete knowledge of the internal process and appeared confident in the accuracy of her work. Below is the basic process I observed followed by a detailed list of my findings:

Receive & open mail → enter bills into accouting system → Send unpaid bills report to CEO to indicate which bills can be paid → Print, sign and mail bill payment checks → Attach check stubs to bills and file

- The process as a whole lacks internal controls, presenting an easy opportunity for processing errors and internal fraud to go undetected for an extended amount of time.
- There were a fair number of interruptions while Clara was entering bills into the accounting system increasing the risk of data entry errors.
- Clara's lack of accounting experience caused her to post several bills to the incorrect GL accounts; rendering system generated financial reports to be inaccurate.
- The unpaid bills report does not provide the CEO with the proper level of detail to make informed decisions.
- A substantial amount of time was spent touching and shuffling paper. I addition to wasting time this increased the risk of documents getting damaged, lost or misfiled.

Recommendations:

- Implement a clear separation of duties by involving others in the process to help ensure security and reduce the potential for errors
- Including project managers in the approval process, allowing them confirm that all materials and supplies billed for have been received and charges are accurate.
- Include accountant or individuals with accounting knowledge in the process to ensure bills are allocated to the correct GL accounts. This will ensure financial reports are accurate and will reduce the need for year-end adjusting entries.
- Provide decision makers with bills details to allow them to make more informed decisions
- Implement a solution for processing electronic payment electronically and storing documents in digital format to save time and eliminate the potential for lost documents.

Our firm has several affordable technology and service solutions that can help to resolve these issues and help to make other processes in your organization more secure and efficient. I will contact you next week to schedule a time to review this report and review some options for solutions.

*Figure 5-1 Sample observation letter*

## Conduct a Survey

Surveying your clients is another terrific way to gather information. Check out these free online applications that allow you to create surveys and collect and analyze the data:

- SurveyMonkey   surveymonkey.com
- Zoho Surveys   zoho.com/survey
- Polldaddy   polldaddy.com
- Zoomerang   zoomerang.com

You should plan your survey before you create it. Fortunately, most of the free online applications provide guidelines and best practices for creating effective surveys. You can use the examples below as a basis for getting started.

- What is the goal of the survey?
    - To determine which clients would a good fit be for:
        - Bill.com
        - Other technology services
        - Assistance with accounting processes
    - To better understand your clients' feelings concerning:
        - Your firm as a whole
        - Individuals within your firm
- Who you will survey?
    - Client type
        - Business tax clients
        - High-net-worth tax clients
        - A specific industry niche
    - Individual type
        - Business owner/CEO
        - Bookkeeper/office manager
- What types of questions you will ask?
    - Open-ended questions that require the respondent to write a comment

- Specific questions that offer yes-or-no, multiple choice, or rating options
- Question with an opportunity for follow up
- What type of incentive you will offer respondents?
  - Gift card
  - Name in a drawing to win a prize
  - Free evaluation (process, technology, etc.)
- How will you explain why you are collecting this data?
  - Example: Our team is in the process of researching some of today's leading technologies for providing better support to our business clients, and for adding value to the services we provide. Please take a few minutes to complete the attached survey. Your answers will provide us with valuable insight and information to help us make more informed decisions. As a token of our appreciation, your name will be entered into a drawing to win...
- What will be the timeframe for the survey?
  - Keep it short, no more than 30 days.
- Plan to resend the survey to non-respondents in advance of the expiration date.

Unlike traditional market-research surveys that gather and analyze information from a large number of respondents, you will use yours to gather information about each client's specific needs. You should plan to review individual responses on a regular basis, and prepare a plan of action for effective follow up.

## How to Deliver an Effective Product Demo

By now you should be able to identify clients' pain points and have a good idea of what services you want to recommend. Now it's time to approach your client and schedule a time to discuss some options. You gather up your laptop and head out to their office, where you log into a Bill.com account and begin demoing the whole process. This, however, is where things can go terribly wrong.

Delivering an effective client demo begins with preparation. Using the information that you have already gathered, prepare a list of their pain points and weaknesses. Add to this list explanations of how you can use Bill.com to solve those problems.

Here are the issues we identified at Mr. Hathaway's home remodeling business, and how implementing Bill.com facilitated solutions:

- Security Risks
    - User roles clearly define who has access to what information and what tasks each individual may perform.
    - Developing a workflow and assigning specific task to individuals are the essence of implementing a clear separation of duties.
    - Approval preferences can be set to require prior CEO approval of scheduled payments.
    - Custom approval policies for amount thresholds and number of approvers can be set to reflect your business needs.
    - Bill.com payments eliminate the need to send paper checks, which pose a greater risk of fraud. Reducing the public exposure of your account information greatly reduces the probability of check fraud.
- Clerical errors
    - The approval feature involves the accounting firm in the review process. This involvement ensures that all entries are accurate and posted to the proper GL accounts. System-generated financial reports will be accurate.
- Inability to make informed decisions
    - With Bill.com, CEOs can review bill details and digital images of all supporting documents with a single click. During this review, they may add notes, approve, or deny the bills.
- Unnecessary paper shuffling
    - Scan, send, and shred. You will never need to touch almost any document again, but will always have access to it. To send a copy to someone else, you can open and print, or send via email.
    - Vendors can email bills directly to your Bill.com inbox.
    - Bill.com payments eliminate the need to print checks and stuff envelopes.

## Building a Demo Company

Now that you know what you want to cover, you can create a demo company to show your clients how easy this will be. Members of the Bill.com accountants' program may create free demo accounts that are prepopulated with inbox documents, bills to pay, and customer invoices. You can edit the settings for these accounts, and add users, documents, and folders to them, creating a more true-to-life experience.

These free demo accounts are a terrific resource, but they do have the following limitations:

- Payment features are disabled
- There are no paid bills, payment confirmations, or cleared check images
- There are no paid invoices
- Accounting software integration is disabled

Because the AP payment feature is disabled, the pay bills page contains a link to a video that demonstrates the navigation of and process for making payments. To show clients the information displayed on the payment confirmation screen, you may want to create a simple document that contains a screen shot, such as shown in Figure 5-2. Remember to include the cleared check image and blur out any information that you want to keep confidential.

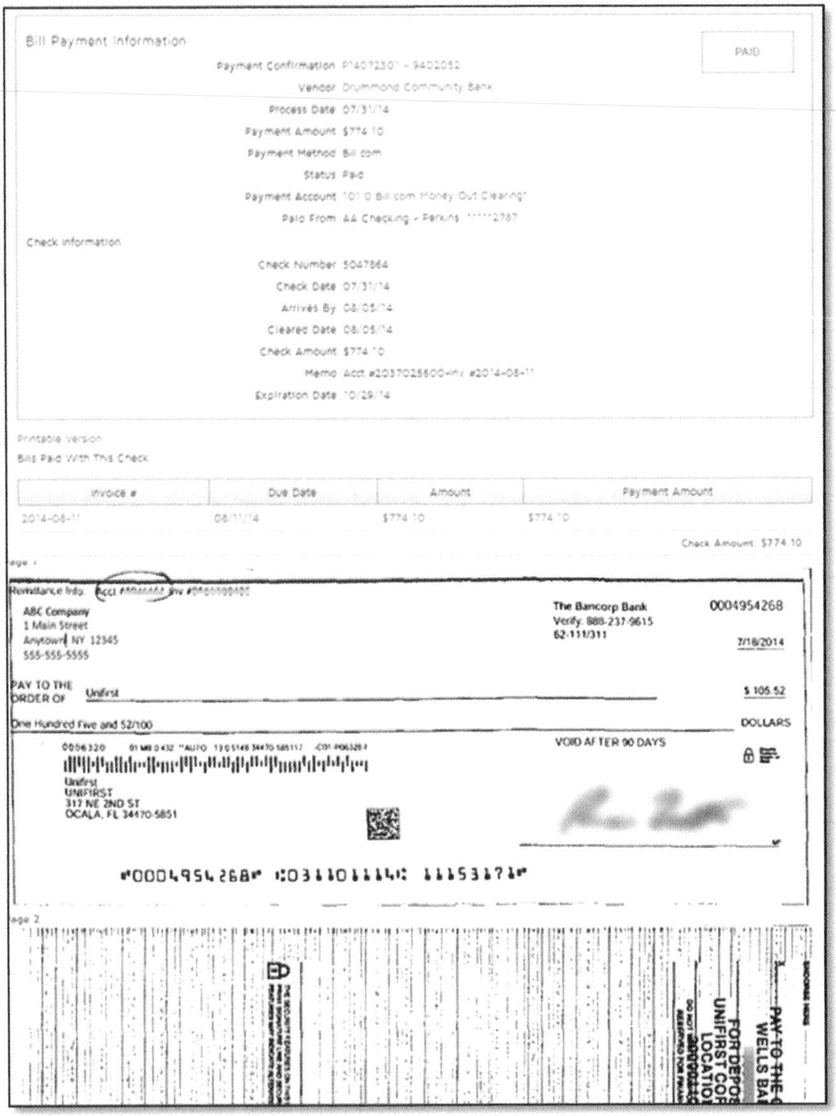

*Figure 5-2 Bill.com check payment confirmation page*

As far as accounting system integration goes, there is really nothing to demo because the sync process occurs in the background. What you can do is explain that transactions will have the same level of detail as though you or the client had entered the directly into their accounting system, giving them the ability to continue generating detailed reports.

Now that you know what the limitations are and how to overcome them, you can begin setting up the demo company in earnest. Remember, you want to show your clients how using Bill.com will eliminate the pain and weaknesses you identified with them. For this reason, I suggest that you set up the account to address those issues and simulate what the client's actual experience will be. You can do this by following these steps:

- Name the demo company the same as your client's business
- Enable only the features that you will be recommending
    - Payables
    - Receivables
- Review the demo account settings and update to match your client's needs
    - Accounting preferences
    - Payables approvals preferences and policies
- Create custom user roles as required
- Add users with appropriate roles
- Add transactions as necessary
- Assign bills to users with approval permissions
- Create a sample folder structure for document storage

Once you have the account set up, do a final check to be sure that:

- Settings are correct
- Each user has action item on their to-do list
- The pay bills page is uncluttered, and has bills with current due dates
- Company documents have been added to the sample folders

Once you have the demo account set up, it's time to present it to your client.

## Presenting the Demo

Now is your time to shine, you have your tools, and are ready to wow your clients. But remember that the demo should not be overwhelming. For that reason, I strongly encourage you to log in as the user you created, with the same permissions as the person you will be demoing to. Do not demo all the functionality as an administrative user. This would be information overload, and make this system seem overly complicated.

For one-on-one demos, encourage your clients to navigate the system as you talk them through the process. If you are presenting to a group, be sure to navigate slowly, and clearly explain each user experience you demo.

Allow time for questions, and if someone asks you one that you don't know the answer to, don't worry. That would be an opportunity to navigate to the support page and show clients how easy it will be for them to find answers on their own.

## Guidelines for Pricing

People often ask me how to price their services. I have even had accountants ask me exactly how much they should charge, when the only information they gave me was a few insignificant details about their clients. Unfortunately, the answer just isn't that easy.

The first thing to do is to first throw out the idea of billing by the hour. Remember, Bill.com is going to help you reduce the amount of time it takes you to do your work. Second, consider the benefits the technology delivers to your clients. They will have added security, digital document storage, and access to their information from any device connected to the internet.

For these reasons alone, it makes sense to price your services according to the value they deliver. And since you will be delivering the same value each month, the adoption of a fixed-fee structure falls right into place.

But how do you determine that fee? Well, there is no one magic formula. Reading through professional publications shows that even the experts don't agree. But they do offer valuable advice nonetheless.

A pricing calculator that calculates a fixed monthly fee for client accounting services is available to members of the Bill.com accountants program. Its output depends on the following:

- Cost of software
  - This include the subscription, user, and per transaction fees
- Cost of labor
  - Calculates the cost based on the amount of time and the billing rate of each person at the firm involved

Once you have calculated these hard costs, you can add in a percentage for value-added features and profit margins. While this may not be the most comprehensive pricing tool available, it does provide an excellent foundation.

## Summary

When it comes to marketing and pricing these services, there is no right or wrong way. What works for a large CPA firm in California may not work for a small bookkeeping firm in Massachusetts.

By positioning yourself as a solution provider who delivers value-added services, your clients will begin to view you as more of a trusted advisor. This may open up additional opportunities as they grow their own businesses or send referrals your way.

Delivering your services for a fixed monthly fee allows clients to budget their accounting services more accurately. This model also facilitates the forecasting of revenues and cash flow for all parties.

# Chapter 6
# Before You Begin...

## Knowledge and Preparation are Key

Before you begin using Bill.com with clients, you should have a thorough knowledge of its functional design. Chances are you will find that the Bill.com workflow differs from what you and your clients understand as typical. This is because Bill.com automates so many tasks, which increases efficiency while reducing the potential for fraud.

In this chapter, you will learn how Bill.com manages AP and AR, and how to develop an effective workflow for you clients. You will also learn in detail how the approval process works, and review some common use cases that demonstrate the power of these features.

To help you prepare for setting up the account, I have included some client set-up resources and an overview of users and user roles.

But before getting to that, here is a review some of Bill.com's terminology, as the system uses some of these words differently than what you may consider usual:

- Workflow – The order in which specified employees perform specified tasks.
- User – An individual who can access Bill.com using a unique user name and password
- Verified user – A user whose identity Bill.com has verified. Verified users may have permission to add bank accounts and make bill payments
- Role – A set of permissions that limits what a user can do and see within a Bill.com account
- Approval – The process in which a user views a bill and all its details
- Approver – A user who has permission to approve bills

- Payer – A verified user who has permission to schedule bill payments
- ePayment – A payment sent or received electronically
- Administrator – A user who has access to all features and if verified can make payments
- Manage – User who have permission to manage can add, edit or delete data

## Understanding the AP Process

The flowchart in Figure 6-1 illustrates how Bill.com processes AP. The shaded boxes indicate tasks that require human interaction.

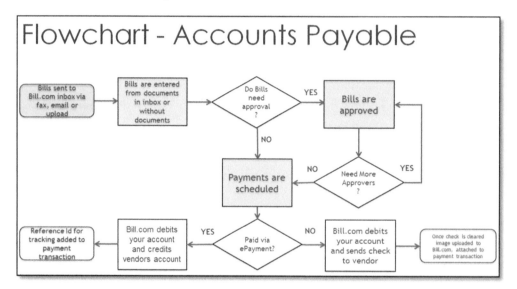

*Figure 6-1 The Bill.com AP process*

As you can see, there are only four tasks that require user input to complete the AP process. They are:

- Sending bills to inbox
- Entering bills
- Approving bills
- Paying bills

Bills and supporting documents can be sent directly to the Bill.com inbox via fax, email, or upload. Because the fax and email methods do not require the sender to have access to a Bill.com account, you can assign this task to administrative staff. Better yet, ask your vendors to send the bills and documents directly to your Bill.com inbox.

Entering bills in Bill.com is pretty much the same as entering them into your accounting system. The only differences are that you will have the bill image on screen and you will need to assign approvers. During this process, the system files the bill and associated details electronically under the vendor's record.

You can route bills to one or more approvers for review and/or authorization prior to scheduling payment. When multiple approvers are assigned the system routes the bills consecutively.

Once you have everything entered and approved (if the bill requires approval) all that is left is to schedule payment. Bill.com allows you to schedule payments for processing later, so you don't need to worry about forgetting to pay them.

## Understanding the AR Process

Figure 6-2 illustrates the Bill.com AR process. The dark blue boxes indicate tasks that require human interaction; the light blue boxes indicate tasks that you can automate.

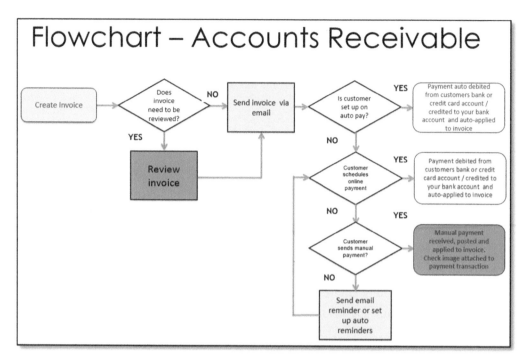

*Figure 6-2 The Bill.com AR process*

As you can see, there are only four tasks that require user input to complete the AR process. They are:

- Creating invoices
- Reviewing invoices
- Sending invoices
- Recording manual payments

Creating invoices in Bill.com is pretty much the same as creating them in an accounting system: Select the customer and enter the invoice details. If someone must review the invoice before it goes out, there is an option to email later. Until it goes out, it remains in the send queue. If an invoice does not require review, the user can select email now.

To review an invoice, open it from the send queue. If you need to make changes, you can edit the invoice and then send it.

When customer chooses to pay electronically, Bill.com automatically deposits their payment in your bank account, and properly applies the payment to the invoice. If a customer sends payment manually, you must record the payment in Bill.com, and apply it to the appropriate invoice. If you received the payment in the form of a check, you can scan the check and attach the image to the payment transaction.

## Overview of the Approval Process

Many people have difficulty understanding the approval process. They think that *approve* means approving for payment. But in fact it means approving the bill. Don't let that confusion deter you, however. With the proper workflow and user roles, the final approver can be the gatekeeper for the money.

Approving a bill in Bill.com is the process in which a user views a digital image of a bill and its associated details. This provides them with all the information necessary to make an informed decision. During the approval process, an approver can add notes to a bill and choose to approve or deny it. Bill.com automatically routes denied bills back to users who have permission to manage bills.

Here are the most common use cases for assigning bills to an approver:

- Confirming that items and services were received in full
- Providing answers to questions noted in a bill
- Reviewing, adding, or editing details such as:
  - GL account or item
  - Class, location, or other dimension
  - Customer or job
- Approving bills that exceed threshold amounts
- Approving bills and indicating there are sufficient funds to pay
- Approving bills and indicating that they are okay to pay when funds are available

The last two use cases come into play when users have permission to pay bills only if the bills have completed the approval process. This is how you can use the role of approver to provide the financial decision maker with a complete view the bill details, and control what bills get paid and when.

## To Approve or Not to Approve

Depending on the size and complexity of a client's business, you may or may not decide to use the approval process. As a guideline, however, if more than two people are involved in the AP process, you should use approvals.

Here are two examples of when you may not want to use the approval process:

Example 1: David Rollins is an independent contractor who does odd jobs and lawn care. He manages all of his own bookkeeping. He sends his bills to his Bill.com inbox as he receives them. At the end of each week, he logs into his account, enters the details from the documents in the inbox, and then schedules the payments.

David does not need to use the approval process because he is the only individual involved in entering the details and scheduling the payments.

Example 2: Maria Fernandez owns a plant nursery that keeps her busy for much of the time. At the end of each day, Maria opens her mail, reviews bill documents, and then sends them to her Bill.com inbox. Gina, her trusted bookkeeper, enters the details from the documents in the inbox. Once a week, Maria logs into Bill.com, considers her available cash, and schedules her bill payments.

Maria does not need the approval process because she reviews the bills as they arrive in her mail, and sends only the ones she approves to her Bill.com inbox.

If Maria were to change her process by having Gina open the bills and enter them, she would want to adjust her Bill.com workflow as well. By setting up herself as the default approver and giving Gina permission to pay approved bills, she would retain control over money movement. This would save Maria even more time, because she would not have to rummage through her mail each day.

## Overview of Users and Roles

Earlier in this chapter, I explained that a Bill.com user is an individual who has access to a Bill.com account by means of a unique user name and password. I strongly discourage sharing login credentials for reasons such as:

- Controls and security are compromised
  - Persons who share logins consequently share permissions, and that could reduce the effectiveness of your controls.
- The audit trail will be inaccurate
  - When users enter or edit transactions, Bill.com tags the changes with the users' name. Sharing logins thus creates unreliable information.
- Important notifications could be overlooked
  - Because Bill.com sends notifications only to the email address associated with a specific user, a user with a shared login could miss important information.

Bill.com automatically assigns the role of administrator to the person who creates an account. Administrators can add additional users and begin the set-up process. When adding a new user, you must enter the user's name and email address. The user's email address will be his or her user name for logging into Bill.com. Bill.com will also use that email address to notify the user of tasks on their to-do list that need attention.

Next, you must assign each user a role. Bill.com provides five user roles; each allows a different level of data access and grants specific privileges. Remember that users with permission to pay must go through a verification process before they can make payments via Bill.com.

Figure 6-3 shows these five roles and provides a brief description of the permissions for each.

| Permission | Administrator | Accountant | Payer | Approver | Clerk |
|---|---|---|---|---|---|
| Approve Bills/Vendor Credits | yes | yes | no | yes | no |
| Manage Vendor | yes | yes | no | no | yes |
| Manage Bill | yes | yes | no | no | yes |
| Record Payments made outside of Bill.com | yes | yes | yes | no | yes |
| Pay approved bills via Bill.com* | yes | no | yes | no | no |
| Pay unassigned bills via Bill.com* | yes | no | no | no | no |
| Pay unapproved bills via Bill.com* | yes | no | no | no | no |
| Manage Company Info | yes | no | no | no | no |
| Manage User | yes | no | no | no | no |
| Sync with Accounting System | yes | yes | no | no | no |

*User needs to go through verification process to pay via Bill.com*

*Figure 6-3 Bill.com standard user roles*

In addition to the five standard user roles, Bill.com provides a Custom Users Roles feature that allows you to define a set of permission specific to your individual needs. You can use the Custom User Role worksheet as a guide for creating and documenting these roles. Once you create a custom users role, you can assign it to one or more users within your account. Keep in mind, however, that any changes you make to that role will affect all users that role has been assigned to. (See page x for more on downloading the supporting documents for this book.)

## Email Notifications

The final step to adding a user is selecting the user's notification preferences. The system suggests a default setting based on the users role, but you can edit that during the set-up. Users can also manage their own email settings at any time.

There are two types of notifications:

- Instant notifications
- Periodic summaries

When selecting instant notifications, be aware that Bill.com sends users an email every time either another user or the system assigns them a task. For account users who handle a fair volume of transactions, these emails can add up. The result is email overload, and users begin to ignore the messages, which could cause them to miss important notifications. To ensure the effectiveness of notifications, be sure to set notification preferences that are appropriate for each user.

The option for periodic summaries is in many cases a better fit. These notifications contain summaries of the tasks that appear on users' to-do lists. You can schedule them for daily delivery, or for specific days of the week or month. For users who have access to multiple accounts and log into Bill.com on a regular basis, the preferred notification strategy is to turn off email notifications completely.

## Gathering the Right Information

Gathering all the information required for company setup in advance facilitates the process. This information includes:

- Company name and address
- List of users
- Accounting preferences
- Approval policies
- Bank account information

Use the client setup checklist to ensure that you have all the necessary information prior to beginning the client setup. See page x for more on downloading the supporting documents for this book.

## Developing Your Own Workflow

Developing your workflow is the most important part of the set-up process. Mapping out your processes helps you to identify the who, when, and why of each process. It also helps in determining:

- The level of access each user will need
- Potential weaknesses in the process
- Whether efforts are being duplicated

For example, Brandon is an accountant. His client, José, is the owner of José's Dance Academy, which has two locations. Brandon will be working with José and Brenda, his in-house bookkeeper, to manage the AP and AR processes.

Each location has a manager who is responsible for approving bills before they get paid. In addition, the mangers are also responsible for ensuring that the students pay their fees on a timely basis.

Because José is busy trying to grow the dance school, he spends a lot of time outside the office visiting schools, social groups, conferences, etc. Brandon has determined that Bill.com will enable him to become more involved in the process. It will also facilitate Brenda's efforts to encourage the managers to approve bills more quickly, and reduce the amount of time she spends printing checks and stuffing envelopes.

Brandon also suggested that the managers use Bill.com to manage AR. This will allow them to automate the invoicing process and set students up on auto pay.

Figure 6-4 illustrates a likely AP workflow for this situation.

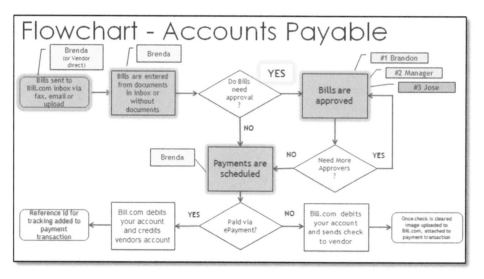

*Figure 6-4 AP workflow for José's Dance Academy*

In this example, Brenda receives, enters, and assigns the bills for approval in the following sequence:

1.    Forward to Brandon to ensure proper account coding

2.    Forward to the location manager to approve bills for his location (each manager will have his own login)

3.    Forward to José to review and indicate they are okay to pay

Once the bills have completed the approval process, Brenda will schedule them for payment. Here are some of the important factors that come into play in this scenario:

- Brenda has permission to pay only completely approved bills.

- An approval policy is in place that requires every bill to have a minimum of three approvers.

- Managers can view and approve only those bills which have been assigned to them. They do not have permission to edit any bill.

- Brandon has permission to edit and/or update bills during the approval process.

- No one can edit a bill after its approval is complete.

- José has view access to everything in the account. He also has permission to pay unapproved bills. This allows him to override the system in the event that Brenda or one of the managers becomes incapacitated.

Figure 6-5 illustrates a possible AR workflow for this situation.

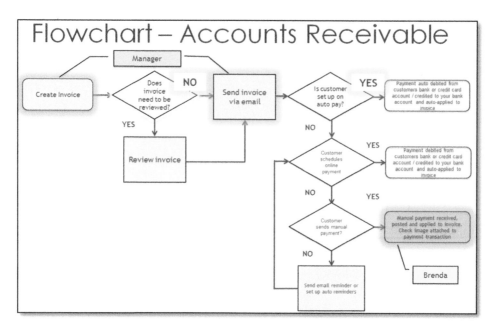

*Figure 6-5 AR workflow for José's Dance Academy*

Managers create recurring invoices for all new students, and set them up on autopay. In the rare instance when a student does send in a manual payment, Brenda receives and posts it.

- Setting up recurring invoices eliminates the manual entry of monthly invoices
- Setting the students up on autopay ensures the timely payment of all fees, and eliminates the need for payment reminders and trips to the bank to make deposits.

Here are a few additional tips for developing effective workflows:

- A single user should not perform two tasks in a row. For example, if a user enters bills, that user should not be an approver, as he or she will have all the necessary information.
- Assign the decision maker as the final approver rather than payer. This will allow that individual to see the bill images, details, and notes added during bill entry or by previous approvers.

- Assign the role of payer to the person who would normally be responsible for printing and mailing the checks.

Remember, Bill.com allows you to work collaboratively with your clients and their staff. By taking the time to develop an effective workflow, you will be able to create a separation of duties and reduce the potential for fraud. Within this workflow, you will assign individual users to individual tasks. You should assign each user a role that permits that user to perform only the assigned tasks.

## To Sync or Not to Sync?

There is no question about it, using the Bill.com synchronization feature is the easiest way to pass information between Bill.com and your accounting system data file. Bill.com support two-way sync with the most popular accounting software applications, including:

- QuickBooks for Windows (all versions)
- QuickBooks Online (Essentials and Plus)
- Intacct
- NetSuite
- Xero

### How the Sync Works

The directional flow of data in the sync feature depends on which version of accounting software you use. For example, Figure 6-6 illustrates information flows between QuickBooks for Windows and Bill.com.

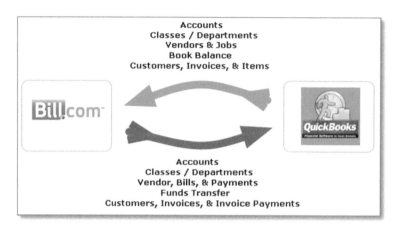

*Figure 6-6 Bill.com sync with QuickBooks for Windows*

In general, information can flow in three ways:

- One-way - Data flows from one place to another.
- Full two-way sync – Data flows in both directions, and can be added or updated in either application. Running sync automatically updates both applications.
- Limited two-way sync – Data flows in both directions, but may not allow for edits in both applications

Understand how the sync function works with your accounting system before setting it up with your Bill.com account. The Bill.com Getting Started - Startup Checklist includes links to helpful information and set-up guides for each supported accounting system. See page x for more on downloading the supporting documents for this book.

Here are a few basic sync rules that you may find helpful:

- Chart of Accounts syncs to Bill.com from all accounting systems
    - Full two-way sync is supported for QB Windows and Intacct
    - One-way sync to Bill.com is supported from all others
- Vendor information is a full two-way sync for all accounting systems
- Bills and bill payments sync from Bill.com to all accounting systems
    - Limited two-way sync of bills is supported only for QB Online and Xero (and cannot be edited in the accounting system)

- Invoices and invoice payments sync from Bill.com to all accounting systems except NetSuite
    - AR is not supported for NetSuite Sync at this time
    - Full two-way sync of invoices is supported only for QB Windows, Intacct, and Xero

The sync method also depends on which version of accounting software you use. For QuickBooks for Windows, Bill.com provides a free sync application that you install on the computer or server that hosts your QuickBooks software. If you are using QuickBooks on a hosted server, you must contact your hosting provider and request the application. A list of hosting providers that support the Bill.com sync application is available from the Bill.com support center.

### About Integration with Other Accounting Systems

Bill.com also offers a robust import/export feature for those accounting systems that do not sync, such as Sage 50 and Thomson Reuters CBS. This feature helps in transferring lists, bills, and payment info to and from Bill.com. Additionally, it allows you to export data that can be formatted for import into your accounting system. For more information about how to export and format data for import into your accounting system, check out the Bill.com support center and search using the keyword export.

## Summary

In this chapter, we covered how work flows in Bill.com and the significance of the primary functions within each process. You also learned how users, roles, and approvals work together in each process, and how to use them to ensure tight controls.

With the knowledge and tools that this chapter provided, you are fully prepared to complete the Bill.com set-up.

# Chapter 7
# Completing the Setup

## Startup Checklist

The Bill.com startup checklist, shown in Figure 7-1, guides users as they set up the account with all the basic information necessary to start paying bills and invoicing customers. The amount of time it takes to complete this process will vary, depending on the features you will be using, but most can complete the process in under a half hour.

The steps are not numbered as you do not need to perform them in any specific order, despite what you may be led to believe. The Bill.com startup checklist indicates completed tasks by a checkmark. You do not, however, need to fully complete the checklist to begin using Bill.com. For example, if you do not intend to use the AR feature, then you don't need to complete the items in the receivables section of the list.

In addition to the basic settings, you will also want to review each section of the settings overview page, and update them on the basis of your client's company preferences and desired workflow.

You can access both the startup checklist and the settings overview pages by clicking on the gear icon, located in the upper-right corner of each page when you are in your Bill.com account.

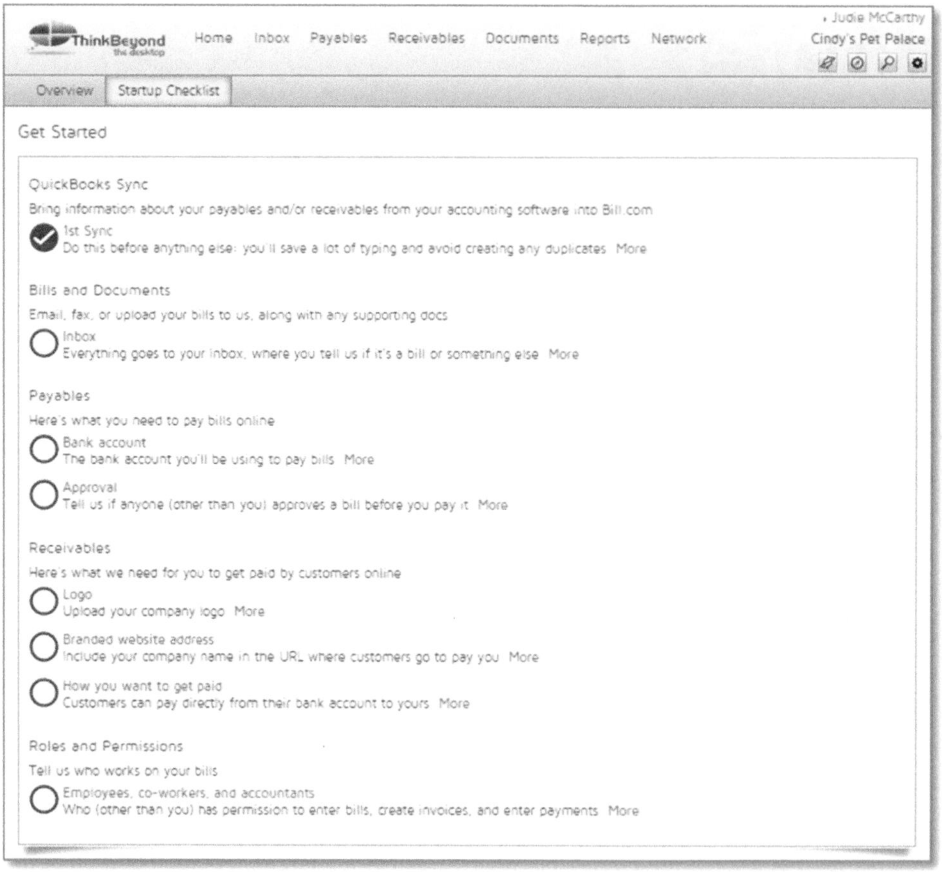

*Figure 7-1 Bill.com startup checklist*

## First Sync

This is the first item on the startup checklist. It will guide you through the process of setting up the integration with your accounting system. The instructions indicate that you must do this before anything else, but that is not necessarily the case. You do, however, want to complete the sync setup before you start entering transactions.

When you first created your Bill.com account, you selected what version of accounting software your client would be using. The system will base the sync setup on that preference. When you first click on the 1ˢᵗ Sync in the startup checklist you will have an option to change that selection if you made a mistake.

When you setup the sync, it is important to connect Bill.com to the actual account or data file that contains all your accounting information. Once Bill.com is married to the data file, it should sync with that file only. Trying to sync with another data file will duplicate information in Bill.com, creating a mess that cannot easily be undone. To help reduce such problems, the sync includes fail-safe checks that will cause the sync to abort if it cannot identify certain objects.

As a precaution after the initial sync is complete, users cannot edit the accounting software selection without contacting support. This is because each brand of accounting software has a different way of identifying or tagging objects. The Bill.com customer support team will guide you through the process or recommend starting a new account.

Once you do complete the first sync, Bill.com will instruct you in mapping the accounts for AR, AP, and the bank accounts.

## Setting Up the Inbox

The inbox setup page, shown in Figure 7-2, is where you will set up the email address and fax number that you will use for sending documents into your Bill.com account. The system defaults to the email address of your company name followed by @Bill.com. You can edit the information before the @ symbol, but it must contain at least eight characters.

The fax number defaults to the area code associated with the company phone number. You can edit this too. If the exchange is not in your local area, it may be necessary to dial the 1+area code when sending a fax.

After you save these settings, Bill.com will display the information on the home page.

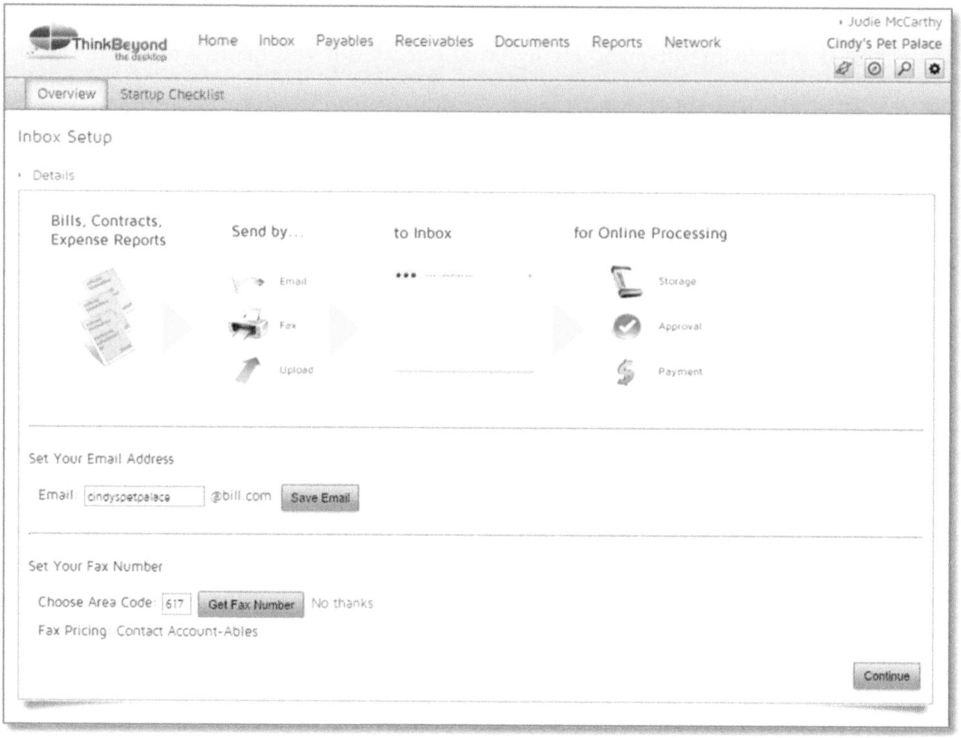

*Figure 7-2 The Bill.com inbox setup page*

## Adding the Bank Account

This is where you link the client's bank account to Bill.com for paying bills and receiving customer payments. It is a three-step process, as shown in Figure 7-3. In most instances, you should have the person who will be responsible for scheduling bill payments via Bill.com perform this process.

As the accountant, however, you may want to complete all the tasks on the startup checklist before adding client users to the account. If that is the case, you can complete the bank account setup, and then nominate other users for verification. That will allow them to schedule payments.

If, as the accountant, you do not want the ability to pay bills on your client's behalf, you can still complete the setup process. After Bill.com verifies an additional payer, you can request your removal from bank account access in

Bill.com. In order for them to remove you, they must have permission to manage users.

Figure 7-3 Bank accounts setup

To begin adding the bank account, you must have the following bank account information:

- Client's bank name
- ABA routing number – from the bottom of a check, not a deposit slip
- Client's account number

If the client is adding the bank account, they should also have their online banking login credentials. This may allow them to instantly verify the bank account so they can start making payments immediately. Without the login credentials, account verification could take one to three business days.

To add a bank account in Bill.com, you do not need to be a signer on the account, but you do need to check the box indicating that your client has given you permission to connect their bank account to Bill.com. You will also need to accept the Bill.com payment terms of service, which you can view in advance by clicking the link.

### *Becoming Verified*

During the bank account setup, Bill.com will attempt to verify your identity. This is not a credit check, and will not appear on your credit report as an inquiry. By requiring user verification, Bill.com protects the bank account from unauthorized impersonators who may be looking to fraudulently gain access.

To begin the verification process, you must enter your residential address, not the address of the business or a post office box. The automated system will search the web for publicly available information about you. If it is unable to access your public record, it may request the last four digits of your social security number as well.

Once the system locates your record, it will present you with three to five questions, such as those shown in Figure 7-4. Once you have correctly answered the questions, the system will prompt you to enter the bank account details.

If you have administrative access to the bank account via online banking, you can enter your credentials to instantly verify the account. Otherwise, you must ask the account owner to check the account in two to three business days, and provide you with the amount of the test transactions that Bill.com posted. Once you have entered the test transaction amount, the bank account setup is complete. Then you can nominate additional payers or begin paying bills yourself.

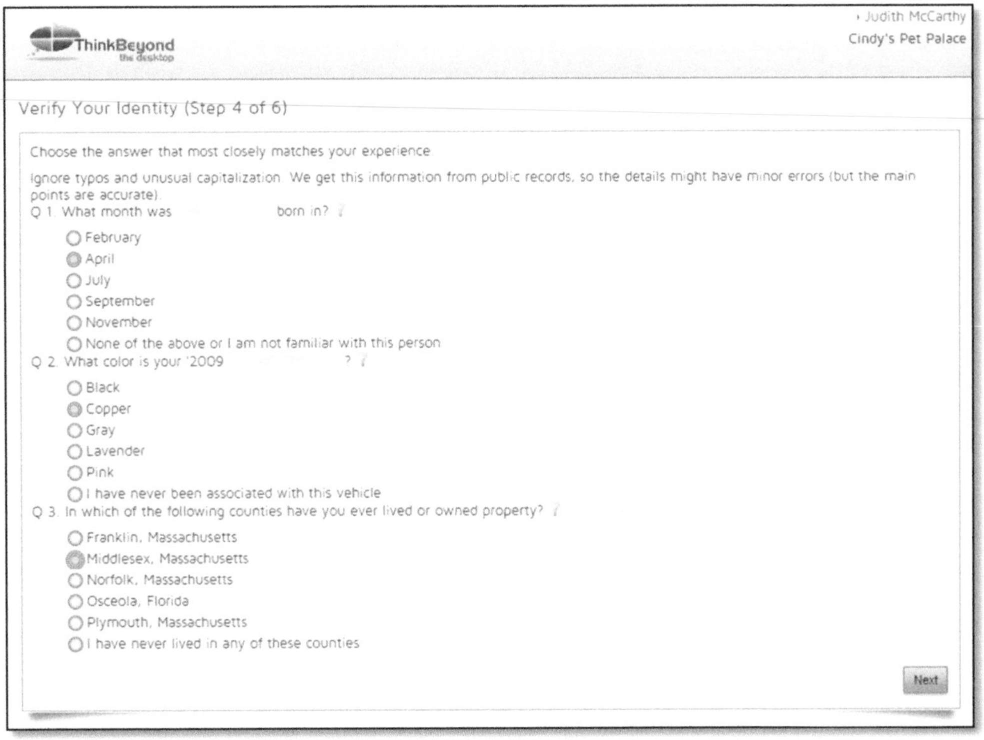

*Figure 7-4 Sample verification questions*

## Setting up the Approval Workflow

This section of the startup checklist asks you to indicate whether or not you will be using the approval process for your AP workflow. If you will be assigning bills to approvers, you should also indicate if and when you will allow changes to bills. The options are as follows:

- Changes are not allowed
    - After approver no. 1 has approved a bill, no changes are allowed.
- Allowed until every approver has approved
    - This means that after approver no. 1 has approved a bill, subsequent approvers or others with the necessary permission could still edit it.
- Allowed anytime

         –   Permitted users may edit bills at any time regardless of whether
               they have been approved or not.

Be aware that users with permission to manage company settings may change this
option at any time. You should consider this implication when you assign user
roles.

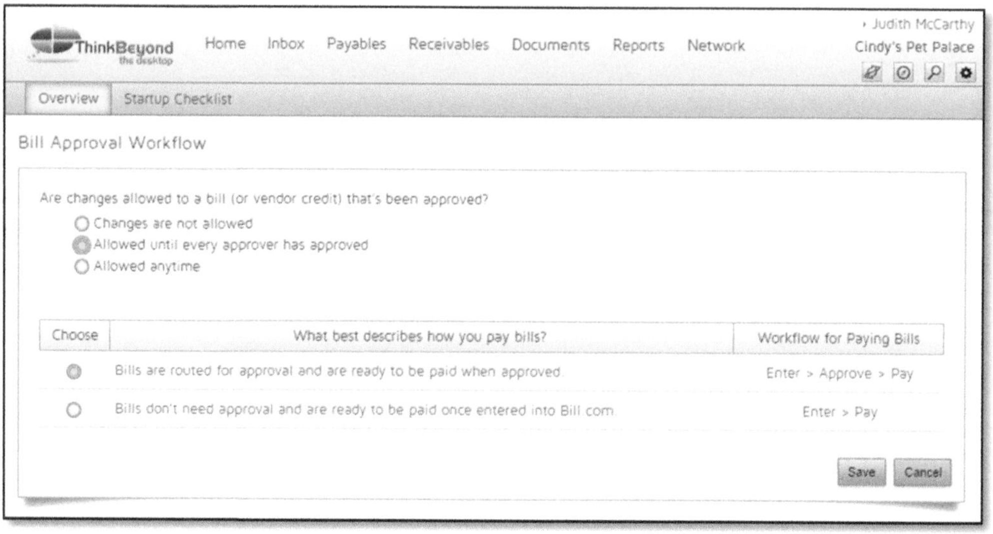

*Figure 7-5 Approval workflow setup*

## Adding a Company Logo

Adding a client's company logo gives invoices a more professional look and
facilitates electronic payments. When you add a logo to an account, it will appear
on all invoices and customer and vendor email correspondence.

Emails personalized by something such as a logo give recipients a sense of security,
and subtly encourages others to join your Bill.com payment network.

To: Clark@PetFoodCity.com
From: Judith McCarthy on behalf of Cindy's Pet Palace

*Cindy's Pet Palace*

Want the convenience of direct deposit payments from us, straight to your bank account? Click the link below to set it up in minutes. It's free to you, Pet Food City.

To get started, click this link.

Thank you,

Judith McCarthy

Please do not respond to this email. This e-mail was sent from a notification-only e-mail address.

© 2007-2014 Bill.com, Inc
app3 37.48.41466 OTID0069-0

Powered by
**Bill**com

*Figure 7-6 Sample vendor invite email with logo*

The logo image must be in JPG, GIF, or PNG format. The area allowed for a logo is 100 pixels wide by 50 pixels high. If you upload a logo that is larger, Bill.com will automatically scale it down to fit. For this reason, Bill.com may not clearly display logos that are square or vertical.

## Creating a Branded Website Address

If your clients will be using Bill.com to manage their AR, you can also create a branded website address, as shown in Figure 7-7. Your clients' customers can use this unique URL to access the portal where they can view and pay invoices.

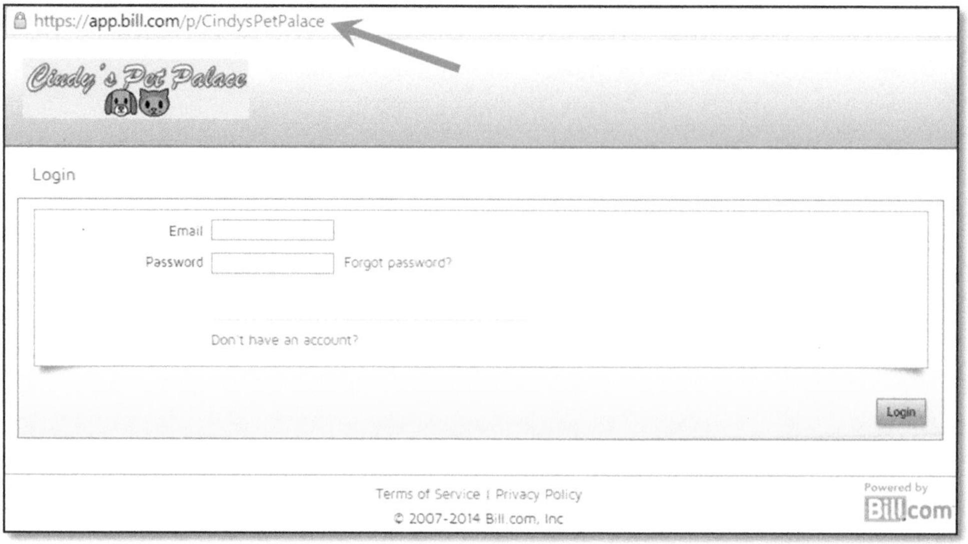

*Figure 7-7 Customer portal login with custom URL*

To create the URL, simply enter at least eight alphanumeric characters in the
space provided as shown in Figure 7-8, and then click the save button.

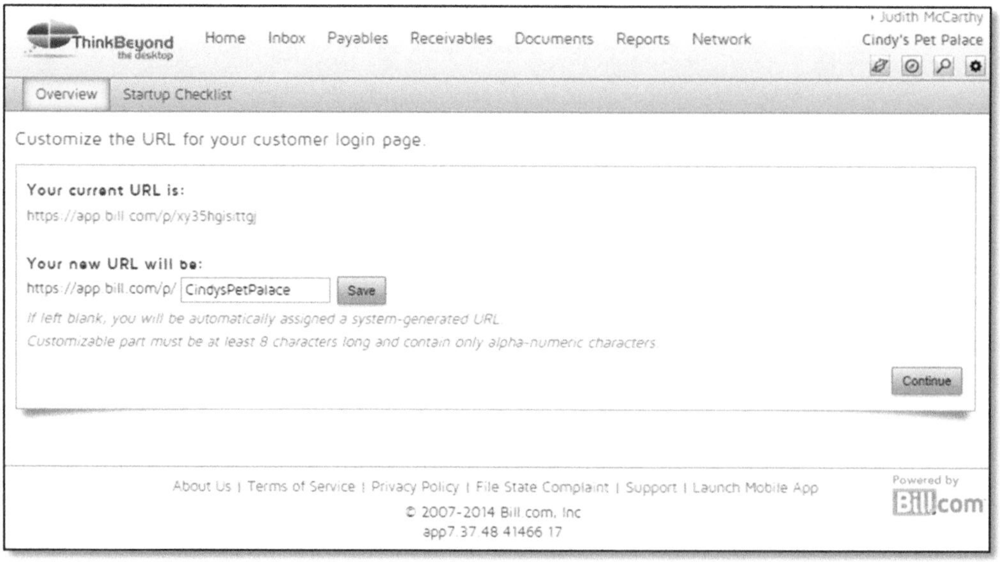

*Figure 7-8 Custom URL setup*

## Setting Up Payment Options for Receivables

This section of the startup checklist may take more time than all the others, depending on what payment options you select. Bill.com provides three options for receiving customer payments:

- ePayment
  - Funds are withdrawn from the customer's bank account and deposited into your client's bank account
- PayPal
  - Customers can remit payment to your PayPal account. This is a convenient way to accept occasional credit card payments if you don't have a merchant account. The setup is free, but standard PayPal fees apply.
- Credit card
  - If your client wants to offer the convenience of credit card payments to their customers, they can set up a merchant service account with Vantage/Paytrace. Bill.com does not support any other merchant service providers for managing credit card payments.

Your client may want to offer multiple payment options to their customers. The setup process for each payment method guides you through all the steps necessary to complete the setup.

To accept ePayment, no additional action is necessary if you have already set up a bank account for paying bills, and your client wants to use the same one. If your client wants to have payments deposited into a different bank account, now is a good time to set up that account.

The PayPal setup is easy and requires only your client's PayPal login credentials. For this reason, you may elect to have your client complete this setup process.

Preparing to receive credit card payments is three-step process, and takes some additional time. To begin, enter the client's estimated annual credit card sales and average charge amount to request an instant quote. Figure 7-9 displays an example quote.

You can print this quote and reviewed with your clients. If they decide to proceed with the setup, they can access an application directly within Bill.com. When the merchant service provider approves the application, they will send an email to the address provided on the application. This email will include instructions for completing the setup.

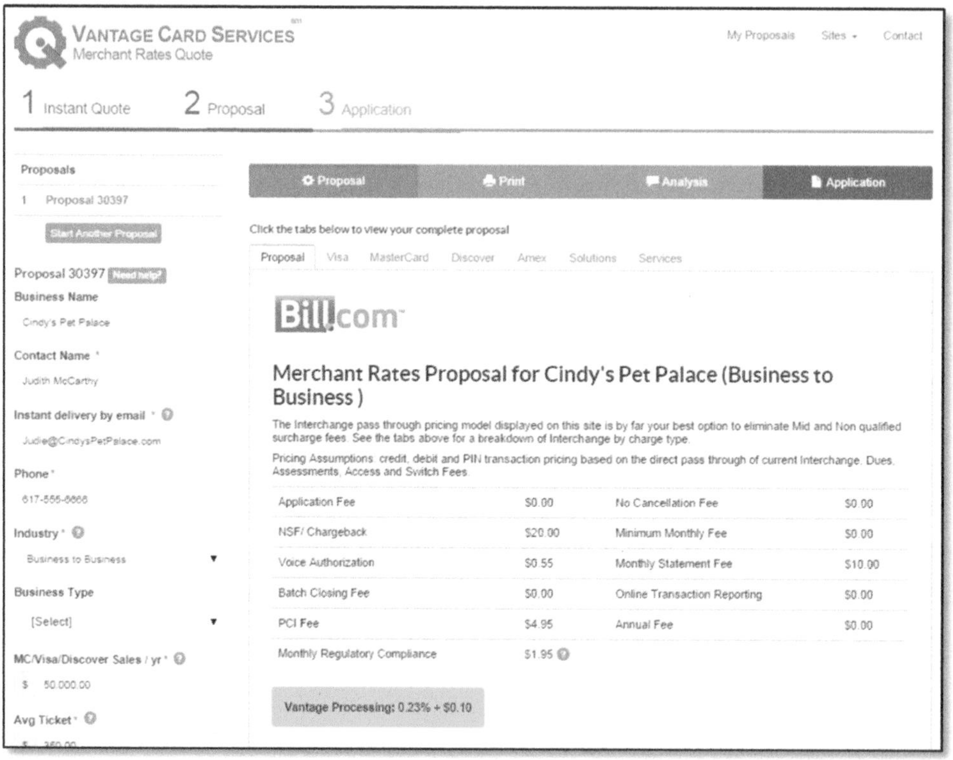

*Figure 7-9 Sample Vantage rate quote*

## Roles and Permissions

This section of the startup checklist is where you can begin adding additional users. Clicking on the link provided redirects you to the user setup page, shown in Figure 7-10. That is where you enter a user's name and email address, and select a role for that user. If the client's workflow requires custom user roles, they must be set up in advance from the permissions section of the settings overview page.

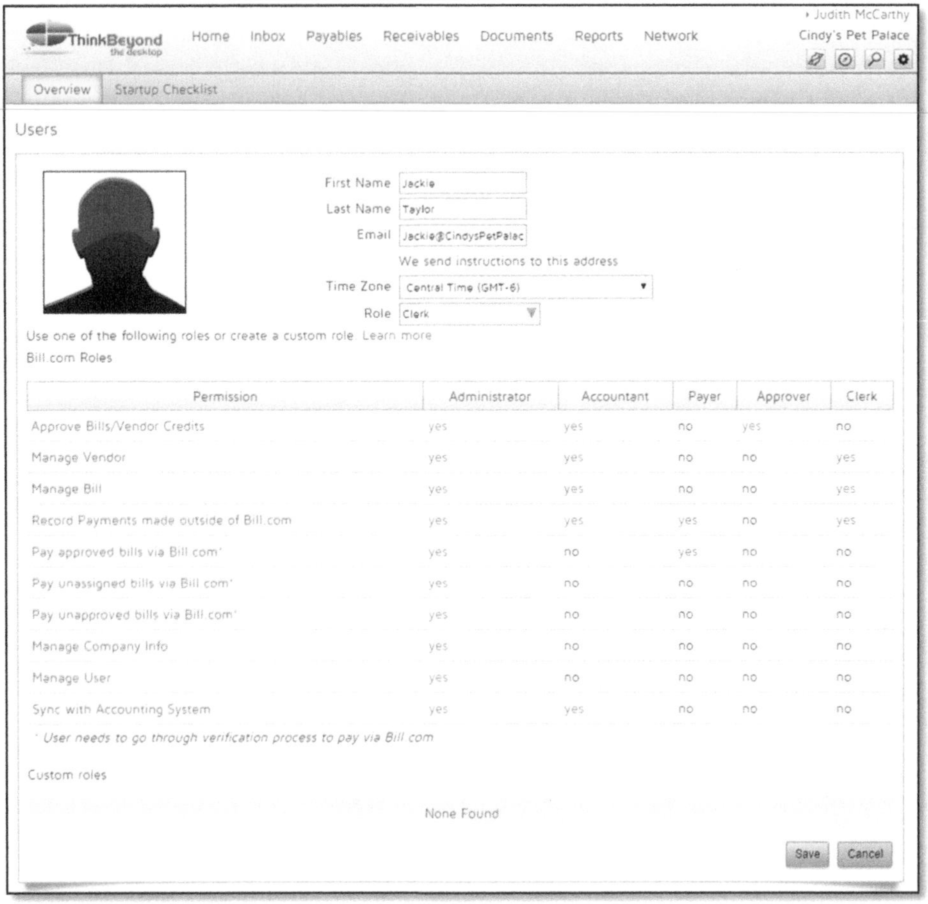

*Figure 7-10 User setup page*

## Additional Settings and Preferences

In addition to the items on the startup checklist, you should review all the settings on the settings overview page, shown in Figure 7-11. Bill.com has organized this page into sections that facilitate navigation. Each of these sections contains links that redirect you to a page where you can view and edit those particular settings. When viewing this page, users will see only those settings that they have permission to view and edit.

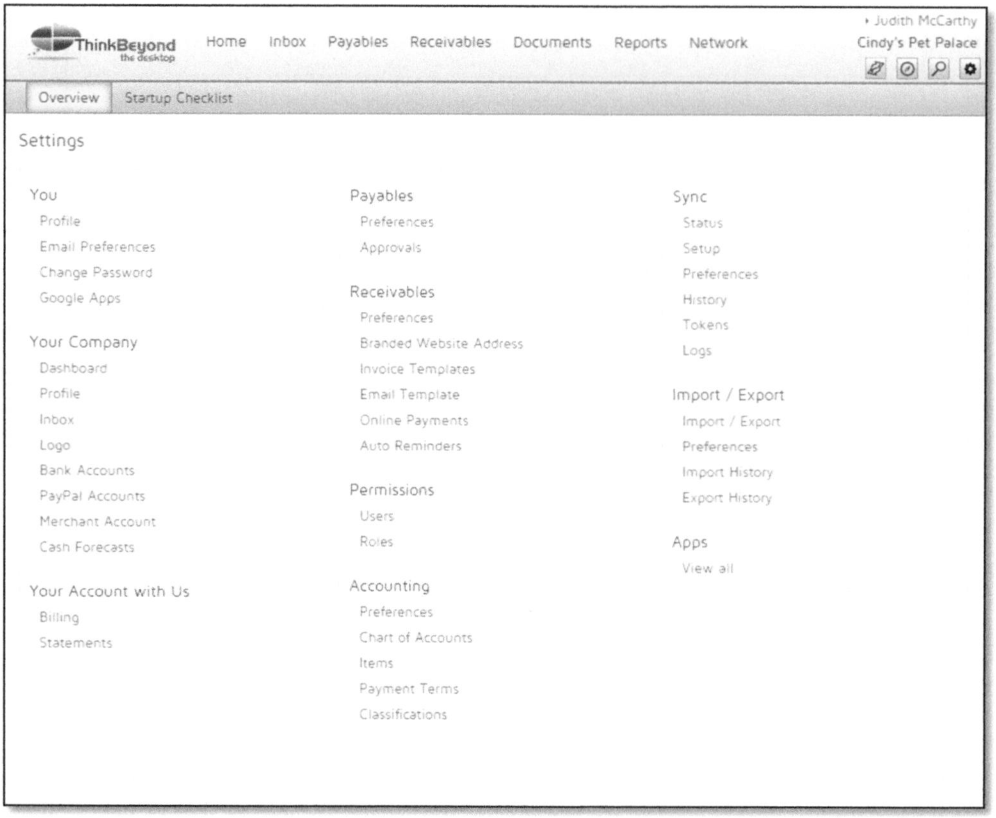

*Figure 7-11 Settings Overview*

## You

This is where you can edit your profile to add a picture, change your password, and update your email preferences. If you need to update your email address, you must contact the Bill.com support team for assistance. Each user can manage his or her own personal settings from this section.

To edit or update settings for another user in the account, select users in the permissions section. From there you can access all pertinent settings from the details link, as Figure 7-12 shows.

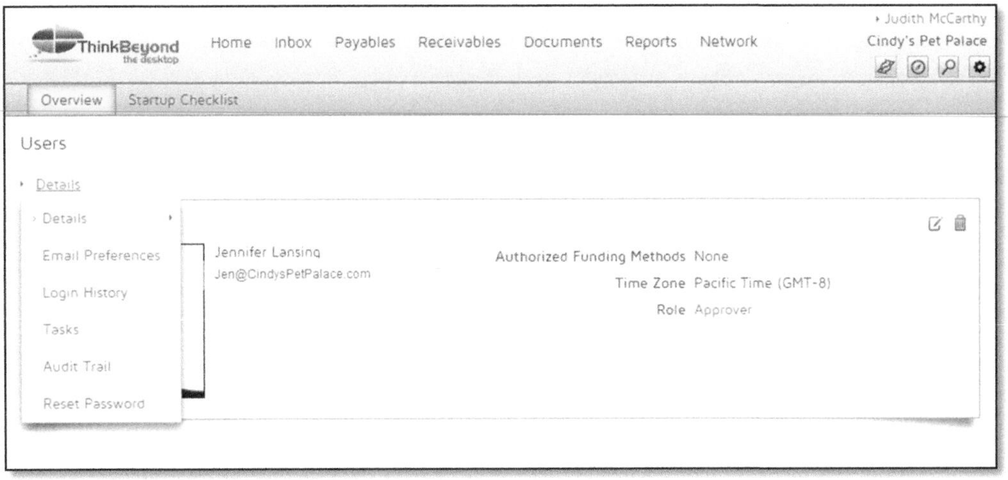

*Figure 7-12 Edit user page*

## Your Company

This is where you can manage all the settings that relate to the company as a whole. These settings include:

- Dashboard – Customize the layout of the home page.
- Profile – Update the company name, address, and phone number.
- Logo – Add or remove a logo.
- Bank, PayPal, and Merchant Accounts – Add or remove accounts.
- Cash Forecast – Customize the types of transactions that you will include in the cash forecast.

## Payables

In this section, you can update the approval preferences and create approval policies. Figure 7-13 displays how, when creating a policy you can specify the number of approvers and identify mandatory approvers for bills on the basis of threshold amounts. There is no limit to the number of policies that can be created, but be aware that only one policy is included in the subscription fee. Bill.com charges an additional fee for each subsequent policy.

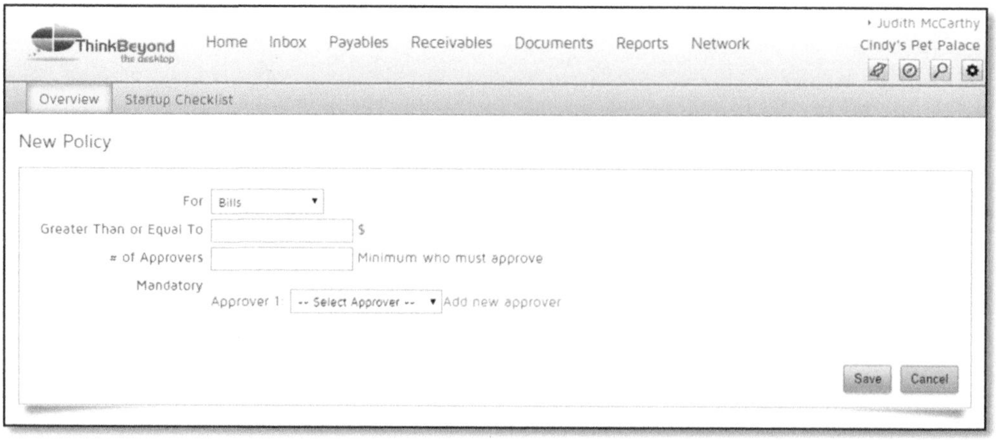

*Figure 7-13 Add a new approval policy*

## Receivables

This section has several settings that we did not cover in our discussion of the startup checklist. These additional settings include:

- Preferences – Select whether or not customers can update or disable autopay.
- Invoice templates – Add new invoice templates or update existing ones.
- Email template – Edit your default email template for sending customer invoices.
- Auto reminders – Allows you to enable and customize up to three customer email reminders that the system will automatically send, based on the criteria you selected, as shown in Figure 7-14.

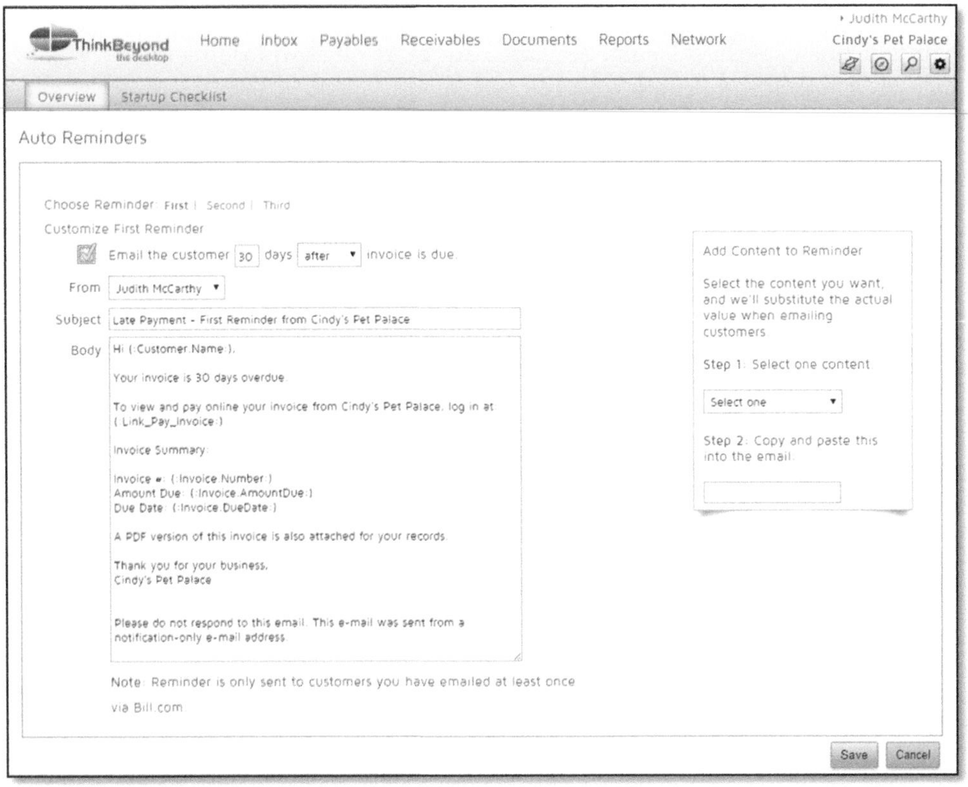

*Figure 7-14 Auto reminders setup*

## Permissions

The permissions section is where you can add users to the account, and where you can view the specifications for each role. This is also where you can create or edit custom user roles, as shown in Figure 7-15.

When adding a new role, the system will prompt you to assign a title, or "name," to it. The role name should not be the same as the user name, but rather a functional title for the person in this role, such as department manager or associate. Another field is available for describing the role. The description should be a summary of the permissions given to users who are assigned this role as shown in Figure 7-15.

Remember, you can use the Custom User Role Worksheet as a guide to prepare for creating a new role in Bill.com. See page x for more on downloading the supporting documents for this book.

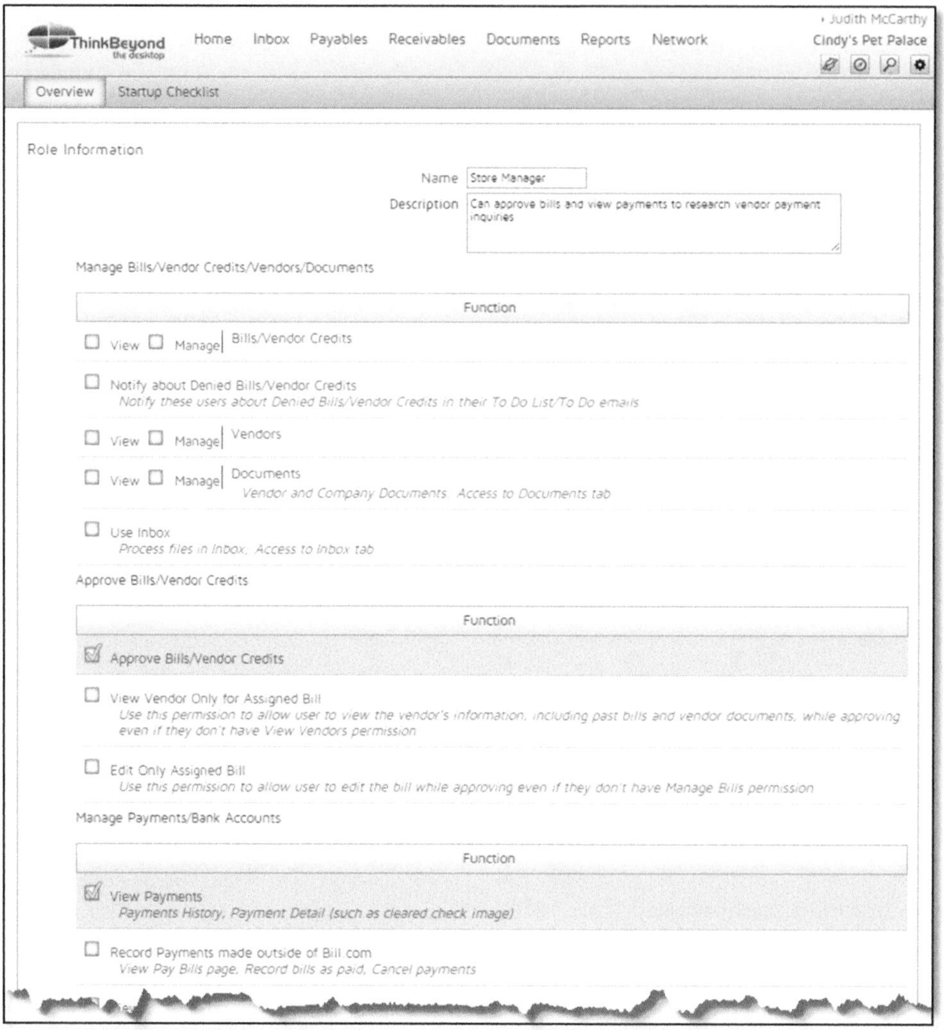

*Figure 7-15 Create or update a user role*

## Accounting

This section allows you to view and manage your lists of objects that you use to classify transactions. Management functions include merging duplicates and activating or deactivating the objects. In addition, you can set other accounting preferences, as shown in Figure 7-16, that we did not cover in the startup checklist discussion.

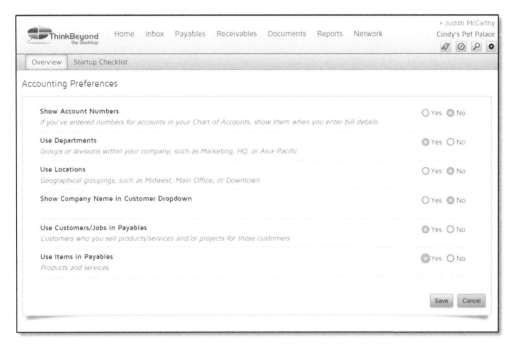

*Figure 7-16 Accounting preferences*

## Sync and Import / Export

The Sync settings allow you to view your sync status, history, and log files in accordance with the accounting software with which you are integrating. Under Preferences you can view and update your sync settings and account mapping as shown below in Figure 7-17.

The Import/Export screen is where you can import and exports lists and transactions if you are not using one of the sync methods. Here you can also import invoices from a .csv file if you are using something other than your accounting system to create them, such as practice management software. Importing invoices allows you to send them and receive payments via Bill.com. After importing invoices, Bill.com syncs to your accounting system so your financial reports are completely accurate.

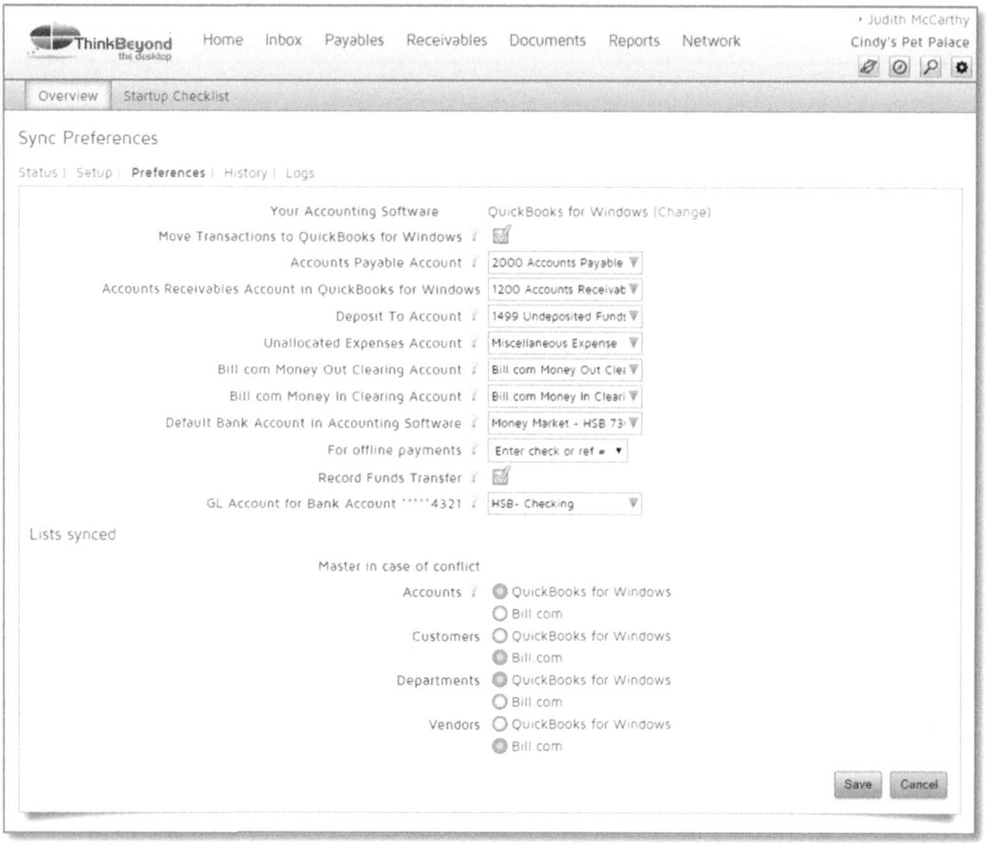

*Figure 7-17 Sync preferences*

## Apps

Bill.com allows you to streamline your workflow by integrating some of the most popular third-party apps, such as:

* Salesforce.com

- Earth Class Mail
- Tallie
- Quote Roller
- Tax1099.com

If you are already using one of these services, this section will walk you through the setup and integration. If you are not, you can click on the app link to learn more about it.

## Summary

By completing the startup checklist and customizing from the setting overview screens, you will be all set to begin using Bill.com with your clients. In addition, you will know how to access each setting in the event that you need to make changes.

Keep in mind that each user's role determines that user's access to the settings. You should carefully consider the potential for unauthorized changes before you allow any user access to the management settings.

# Chapter 8
# Bill.com Best Practices

In addition to helping you understand the technical aspects of Bill.com, I am thrilled to share the system's best practices with you. These techniques will make using Bill.com easier and more efficient for you and your clients alike.

## Accounts Payable Best Practices

### Managing approvals

The approval process in Bill.com is an awesome feature that ensures proper entry and validity of bills. It also ensures tight internal controls that can greatly reduce the potential for internal fraud. Here are some best practices to help you use the approval process in Bill.com effectively.

### Approval Sequence

You should approve bills in a proper sequence when there is more than one approver. For example, if the business owner will be using the approval function to indicate that he or she wants to schedule a payment, he or she should be the final approver. If the accountant is involved as an approver for reviewing entries to ensure proper account coding, you may want to assign the accountant as the first approver.

If approvers will be adding notes during the approval process, they must remember that only the subsequent approver(s) and the payer will see the notes. If an approver needs to communicate information to the bill manager or a previous approver, they should add the note and then deny the bill. Denied bills return to the beginning of the process. This enables the bill manager to read the note, follow the instructions, and then send it off for approval again.

### Other Reasons for Denying a Bill

In most instances, the bill manager is responsible for the proper account coding and entry of bill details. For this reason, I strongly discourage giving approvers, other than the accountant, permission to edit bills.

If during the approval process an approver identifies an improper entry, he or she should append a note indicating the problem, and deny the bill. This allows the bill manager to review the notes, make the appropriate edits, and send the bill on for approval.

Erroneous data entry is probably the most common reason for denying a bill. Here are other common reasons for doing so:

- The items or services have not yet been received
- The amount of the bill differs from the amount quoted by the vendor
- The bill is a duplicate

### Eliminating Approval Bottlenecks

To ensure the timely payment of bills, you should eliminate bottlenecks in the approval process. The best place to view the status of bills pending approval is from the payables overview page.

On that page, you can see any bills that are waiting for approval and whose approval they are waiting for. To remind approvers that they have bills to attend to, you can either speak to them at their desk or send a friendly email reminder via Bill.com. If they have multiple bills to approve, in most cases a single reminder will suffice, but feel free to send as many as you want.

Here is how to send reminders to approvers:

- From the payables overview page, click on the approver's name under the waiting for approval (by approver) section. This will display the complete list of bills waiting for his or her approval.
- Click on the invoice number. This will direct you to the invoice image and any summary information.
- From the bill details link near the top-left corner of the document image, select approvers then click send reminder email.

## Setting Up Vendors to Receive ePayments

The fastest, most secure, and cheapest way to pay bills is through ePayment, but it can sometimes be difficult to set up. There are three different ways to set up vendors for ePayment. They are:

- Find matches
- Invite vendors
- Manual set up

When using the find matches option, you will search for matches in the Bill.com directory. This directory consists of larger corporations, such as financial institutions and credit card companies, insurance providers, communications providers, and utility companies.

To get the best results, you should have your complete account numbers entered into the vendor records. The vendor list displays a column for account number, so you can review the complete list and update them as needed. If you have multiple accounts with a single vendor, you should replicate the vendor for each account. For easy identification, add the last four digits of the account number to the end of the vendor name. This will facilitate entering bills or researching inquiries.

To invite vendors, you should have a valid email address that delivers messages to an individual who has permissions to add the company's bank account details. This is important, because you don't want your electronic bill payments to be deposited into the AR clerks' personal bank account. By the time you figure out this kind of mistake, he or she may be in a foreign country.

Even if you have a valid email address, recipients are often hesitant to accept the invitation, fearing it is a phishing scam. To overcome that obstacle, you should start by sending an informational email to vendors, as shown in Figure 8-1.

Such an email can serve two purposes. The first is to alert them that an invitation is coming their way and to inform them that ePayments mean faster payments. The second is to let them know that they can send bills directly to your Bill.com inbox, saving them time and money.

> Dear Vendor,
>
> We have recently moved to the cloud and implemented Bill.com for managing our bills and payments. This secure, on-line system simplifies the accounts payable/accounts receivable process, saves money, and is environmentally friendly.
>
> **What does this mean to you?**
>
> - You will now be able to fax or email statements to us.
> - You will save time, paper, and postage.
> - You can set up your own FREE account so that you receive payment FASTER!
>
> **What do you need to do?**
>
> - Email statements as attachments to: xxx@bill.com or
> - Fax statements to: xxx-xxx-xxxx
> - Wait for your email from Bill.com regarding setting up your own account. Sign-up and get paid FASTER!
>
> Sincerely,
>
> *Business Owner*

*Figure 8-1 Sample vendor notification*

When all else fails, you can manually set your vendors up to receive ePayments by calling them and requesting their bank information, or by sending a carrier pigeon to retrieve it.

## Managing Recurring Bills

You can use this feature to enter recurring bills for either fixed and varying amounts. It can also remind you of bills that will be coming due soon. We find this especially helpful for clients who prefer to receive electronic bill reminders from their vendors.

Setting up a recurring bill, as shown in Figure 8-2, for the amount of $0.01 and assigning the bill manager as first approver notifies them to either update the amount or log into the vendor website and retrieve the statement. After the statement arrives in the Bill.com inbox it can be attached to the existing bill, which the approver can then update with the correct information and amount.

Note: Bill.com will calculate the bill date on the basis of the due date minus the vendor's payment terms. If you have not set up payment terms for the vendor, then the bill date and the due date will be the same.

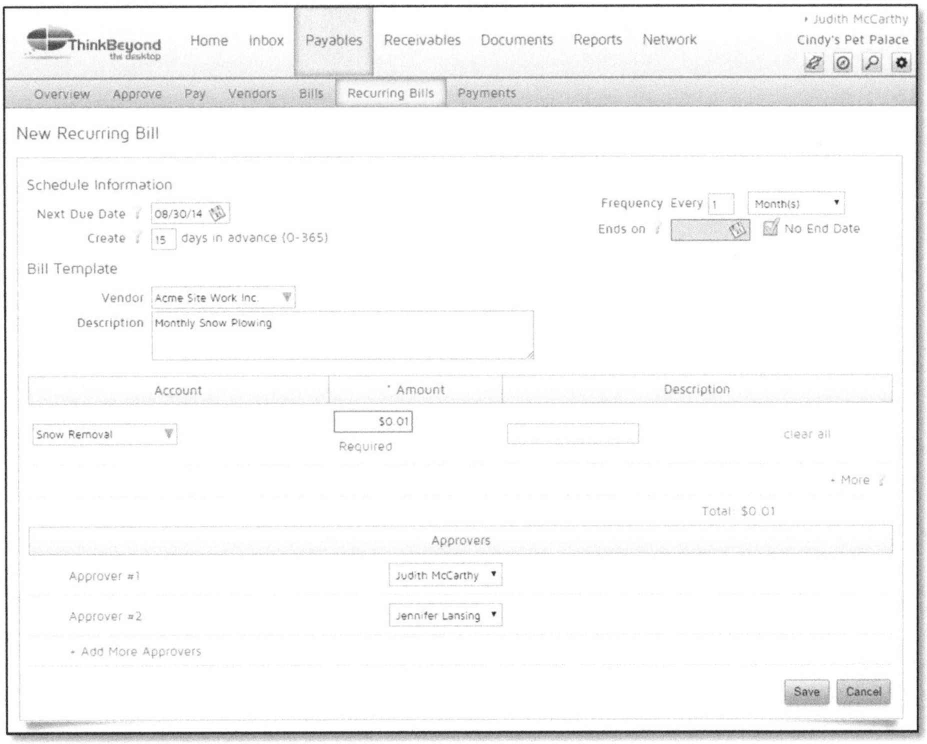

*Figure 8-2 Recurring bill setup*

## Handling Lost Check Payments

Unfortunately, you cannot avoid lost check payments, whether because the cause was the mail truck catching fire on the highway or the vendor's dog eating the check. Most vendors who do not receive payment will call and ask for it. But even if they don't, Bill.com will let you know if a check goes uncashed for 20 days of its issue.

In such an event, the system will assign a task to the to-do-list of users verified to make payments via Bill.com. Like always in Bill.com, clicking the link takes you to the screen where you can manage the task. The page provides complete instructions for voiding the check and reissuing a new payment, as shown in Figure 8-3.

This situation offers an opportunity for you to remind your vendor that ePayments cannot be lost, stolen, or eaten. This may be just what they needed to get them on the ePayment bandwagon.

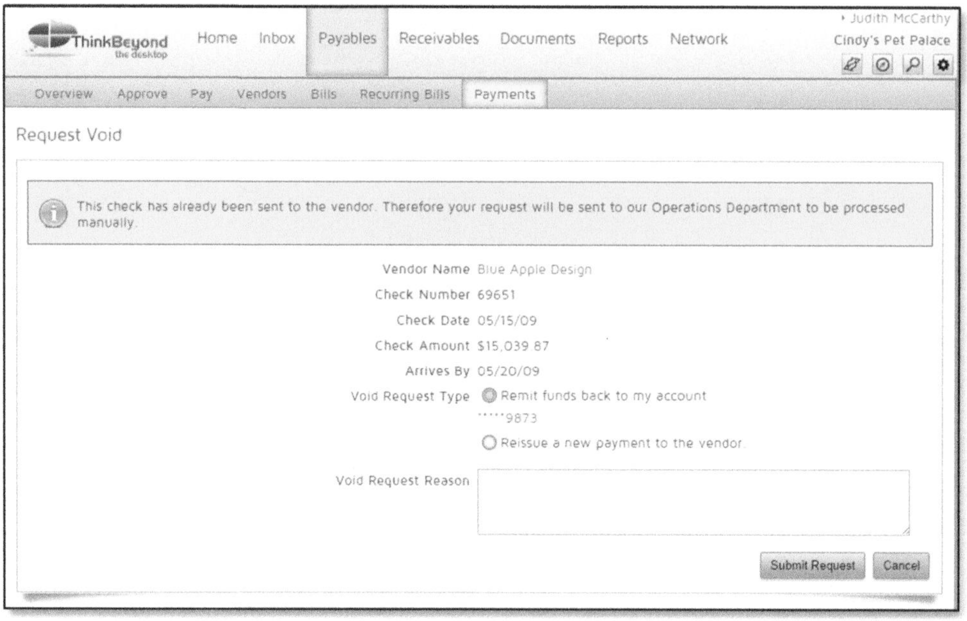

*Figure 8-3 Void check request*

## Writing Off the Balance of a Partially Paid Bill

When scheduling bills for payment, you can enter a partial payment amount, leaving the unpaid balance for payment at a later time. If for some reason at a later time, however, you decide that you are not going to pay the balance, and try to edit the bill amount in Bill.com, you will find that you cannot. But don't worry; there always is a way.

From the Pay Bills Page you will see the partially paid bills listed at the bottom. To write off the balance due and adjust the bill to equal the amount already paid click on the **Paid** link, as shown in Figure 8-4.

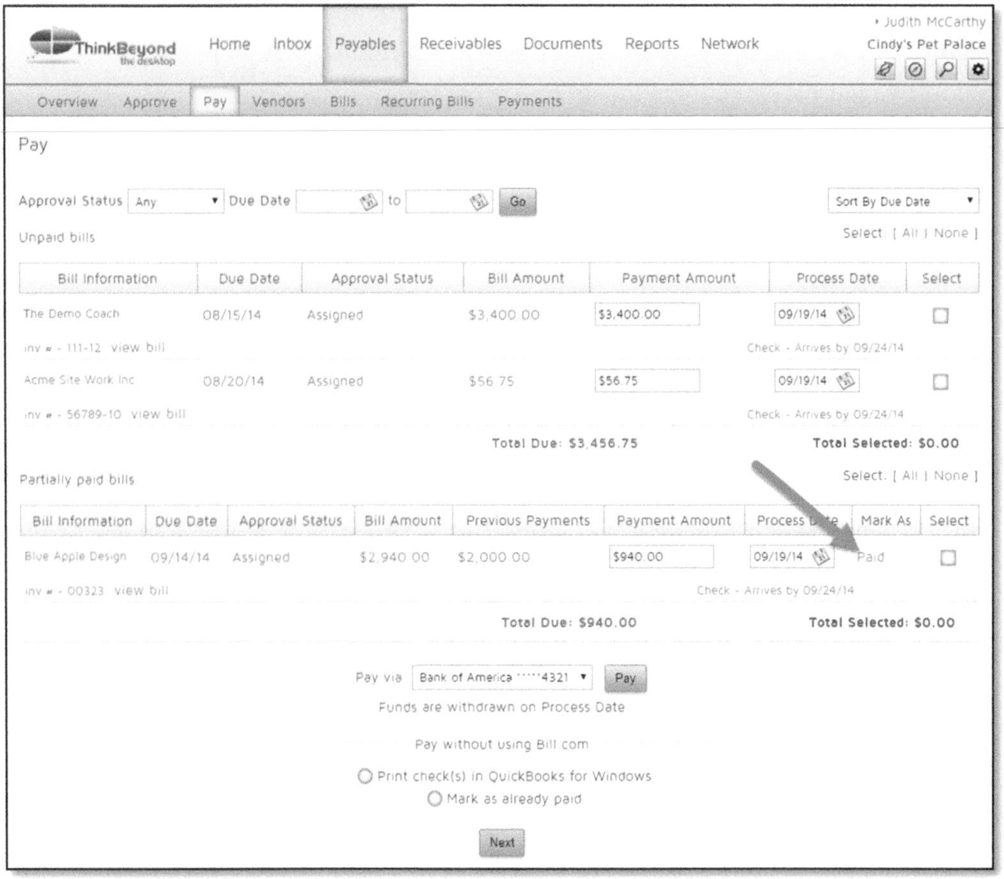

*Figure 8-4 Write off balance of partially paid bill*

## The Bill.com Money Clearing Accounts

When you integrate Bill.com with an accounting system, it automatically creates two new accounts:

- Bill.com Money In Clearing
- Bill.com Money Out Clearing

When syncing with an accounting system, Bill.com posts all payments, by default, to the appropriate clearing account as of the payment process date. When the sync occurs on or after the payment process date, the system automatically creates an offsetting journal entry to post the batch amount to the appropriate bank account register. For accounting systems, such as Xero and NetSuite, that do not support automated journal entry, users should post it manually.

Clearing accounts exist to facilitate reconciliation. When you receive your bank statement, you will see that it contains only the batch amount of all payments processed for a particular date. The clearing accounts also help to identify payments that you made or received via Bill.com.

Many QuickBooks users are not comfortable with this concept; they prefer to see all individual payment transactions in a single register. For such users, I suggest nesting the bank and clearing accounts under a common parent account, as shown in Figure 8-5. The parent account register will contain the transaction in all of the subaccounts. When you reconcile the bank account, you will actually reconcile only the subaccount. But remember: when you use subaccounts, you should not post transactions to the parent account.

| NAME | TYPE | BALANCE TOTAL | ATTACH |
|------|------|---------------|--------|
| CHECKING | Bank | 85,432.46 | |
| Bank of America Checking | Bank | 86,017.46 | |
| Bill.com Money Out Clearing | Bank | -585.00 | |
| Bill.com Money In Clearing | Bank | 0.00 | |

*Figure 8-5 Nested accounts*

# Accounts Receivable Best Practices

## Automating Receivables

Almost nothing is better in business than having money automatically appear in your bank account. One thing that is, however, is having this happen without having to create invoices, run to the bank with deposits, and chase customers down for money.

If you or your clients collect fixed fees on a regular basis, Bill.com allows you to automate the entire process. It begins with setting up recurring invoices, and marking them for automatic email delivery a few days in advance of the due date. You can do this on the recurring invoices page under receivables. Assigning autopay to those customers ensures that your will receive payment on time.

You can set up autopay from the customer's record by clicking on the payment setup link. The first thing that you will need to do is confirm that you have your client's authorization to remove money from their bank or credit card account. You should get that authorization in writing, as shown in Figure 8-6.

After you have confirmed the authorization, enter the bank or credit card details. Then you can then go back to payment setup, select automatically pay bills, and complete the required fields, as shown in Figure 8-7.

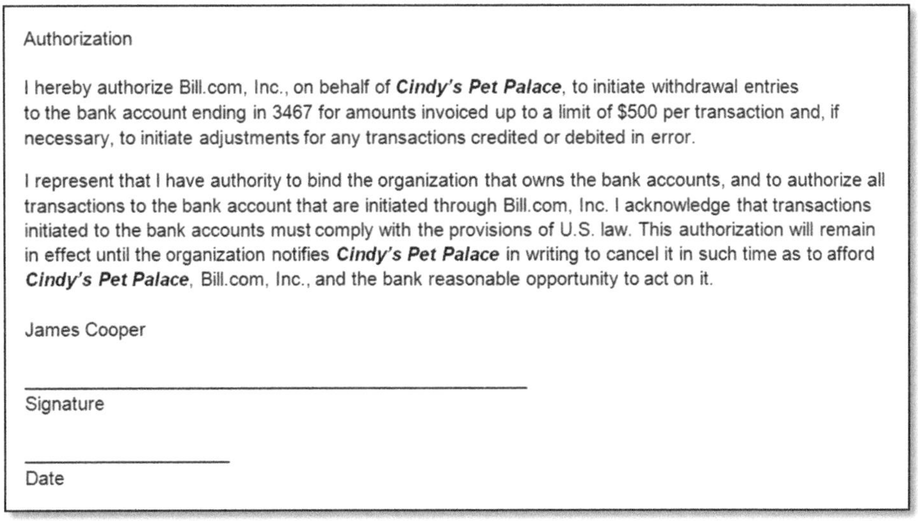

---

Authorization

I hereby authorize Bill.com, Inc., on behalf of **Cindy's Pet Palace**, to initiate withdrawal entries to the bank account ending in 3467 for amounts invoiced up to a limit of $500 per transaction and, if necessary, to initiate adjustments for any transactions credited or debited in error.

I represent that I have authority to bind the organization that owns the bank accounts, and to authorize all transactions to the bank account that are initiated through Bill.com, Inc. I acknowledge that transactions initiated to the bank accounts must comply with the provisions of U.S. law. This authorization will remain in effect until the organization notifies **Cindy's Pet Palace** in writing to cancel it in such time as to afford **Cindy's Pet Palace**, Bill.com, Inc., and the bank reasonable opportunity to act on it.

James Cooper

_____
Signature

_____
Date

---

*Figure 8-6 Sample autopay authorization*

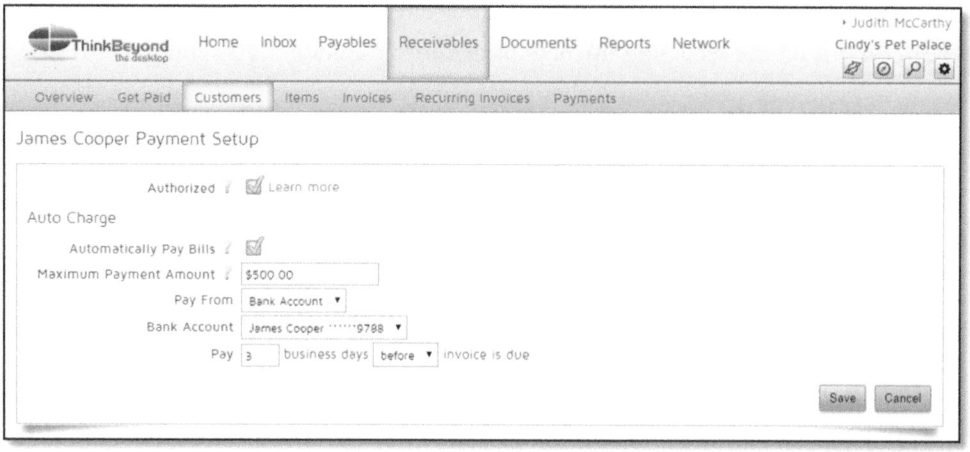

*Figure 8-7 Autopay setup*

As an alternative, your customers can set up autopay from their portal. To ensure that they do not disable the auto pay feature you can lock this information, which then requires them to contact you directly to discuss other payment options.

## The Hidden Secrets of the Customer Portal

The customer portal is a Bill.com hidden gem. You really don't hear much about it, but it has some awesome capabilities.

In addition to being able to create, view and pay invoices, customers can communicate with you or your clients about specific invoices or for general inquiries.

When a customer posts a note in their portal, the system sends an email notification to users in your account who have permission to manage invoices, as shown in Figure 8-8. This email contains the note and a link to view it and/or reply from within Bill.com. The system handles the reply to the customer in exactly the same way. The system permanently posts all notes and replies with a date and time stamp in the customer's record. This is an easy way to document all customer correspondence in a centralized location.

> To: Judith McCarthy
> From: notificationsonly@hq.bill.com
> Subject: James Cooper sent you a message
>
> *Cindy's Pet Palace*
>
> Hi Judith McCarthy,
>
> James Cooper sent you a message:
> "I would like to order 2 reflective cat collars"
>
> To reply, click:
> https://app.bill.com/DirectLogin?email=judie@thinkbeyondthedesktop.com&url=
> %2FCustomer%3Fid%3D0cu01BYFBTYOWBG4p8i3%
> 26orgId%3D00801KCWPHERPVFHqdxu
>
> Have questions? Sign in at our website, then contact support.
>
> Thank you,
> The Bill.com Team
>
>
> Please do not respond to this email. This e-mail was sent from a notification-only
> e-mail address.
>
> © 2007-2014 Bill.com, Inc
> app7.37.48 41466 OTID0063-0

*Figure 8-8 Email notification of a posted note*

In addition to facilitating communication with customers, the portal also allows you to share documents with them. This is a handy place to store shared documents, such as contracts and/or price lists. When attaching a document to an invoice or other communication, you can mark it as public or private. If you attached a document to a customer record and mark as private, the customer cannot view it from within their portal.

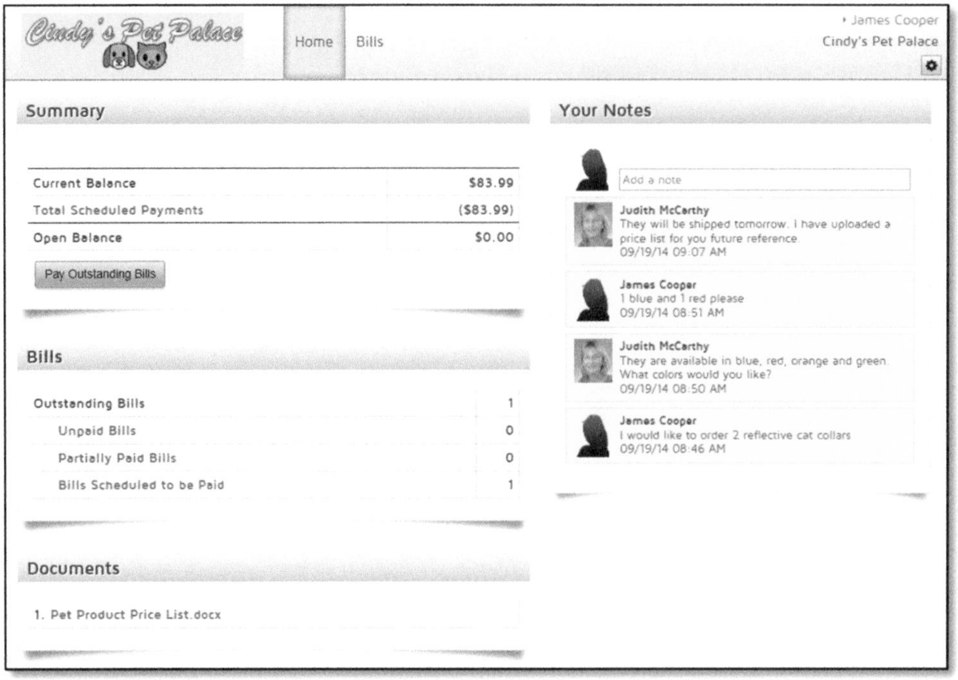

*Figure 8-9 Customer portal, with notes, summary, bills, and a document*

## Cash Forecast

The Bill.com cash forecast tool, shown in Figure 8-10, allows permitted users to view their forecasted balances out to three months in advance. After you enter in a beginning balance, or sync it in from the accounting system, Bill.com generates a forecast that can include both Bill.com and manually entered forecast amounts.

The terrific thing about this tool is the ability to select what types of transactions you would like to include, as shown in Figure 8-11. In addition, you can manually enter forecasted amounts for transactions that do not go through Bill.com, such as daily cash sales, payroll, or automatic debits.

I must admit that the process for entering manual transaction is a bit clunky. For this reason, I suggest you either batch them by date or week, or use the clone feature. You can find the clone feature through the details link while viewing a forecast transaction, as shown in Figure 8-12.

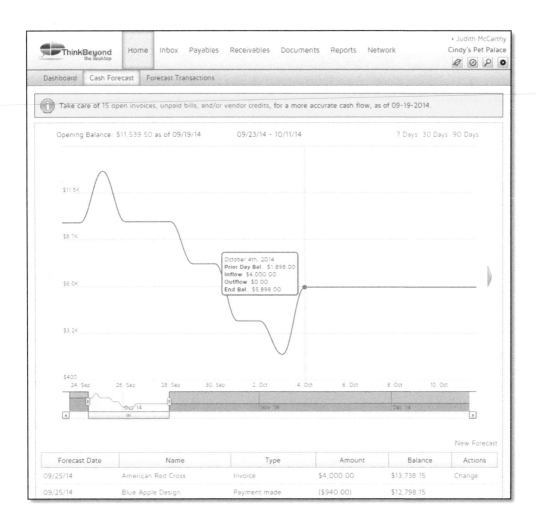

*Figure 8-10 Cash forecast*

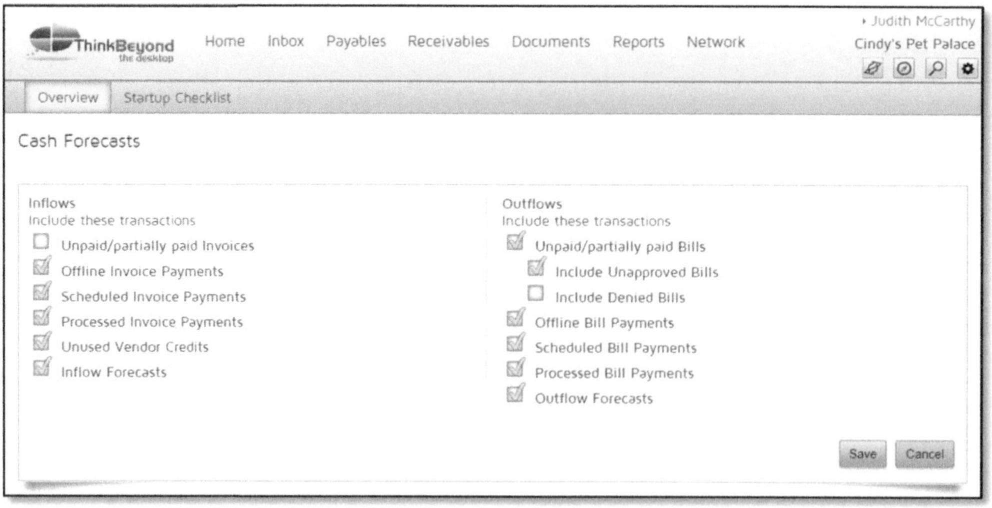

*Figure 8-11 Cash forecast settings*

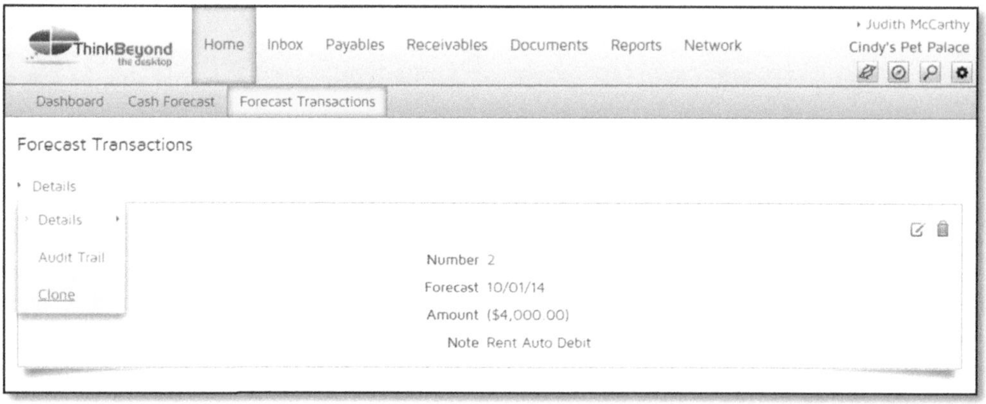

*Figure 8-12 How to clone a forecast transaction*

## Summary

Putting best practices to use will help you use Bill.com more effectively. These hidden gems add additional value that will benefit not only the firm but their clients, vendors, and customers alike.

# Chapter 9
# Conclusion

I hope that you have found this book to be valuable and informative, and have even enjoyed reading it. With a thorough understanding of what Bill.com is and how it works, you should be well prepared to get started.

Here are some final takeaways concerning Bill.com and other cloud-based applications. I hope that they will help to grow your practice.

- Invest time in understanding how to use new applications before deploying them to clients.
- Select applications that will support the masses, not just fix a problem client.
- Understand each application's support model and know how to get help.
- Don't let your clients dictate the tools you use and how to do your work.
- Let go of clients who don't trust your ability to make smart decisions.
- Unless you are a clock salesperson, you shouldn't sell time.
- When in doubt, ask your peers. But remember, everyone has an opinion.
- Don't be a clone. Build your own brand based on who you are, not on who you think you should be.

Thank you for reading this book. I wish you much success as you embark on your journey of growing your practice with Bill.com.

# About the Author

Judie McCarthy, accounting technology consultant and cloud evangelist, has more than 15 years' experience in the world of small business accounting. She is the founder of Think Beyond the Desktop, a professional service firm that provides remote accounting services to small businesses. In addition she consults with accountants and bookkeepers to guide them through the process of transitioning to the cloud to support their clients and grow their practices.

Judie is the original Bill.com Guru and former Director of Accountant Relations for Bill.com. While there she used her in-depth knowledge of accounting processes mixed with her product expertise to help accountants gain firm wide adoption and successfully implement Bill.com. In addition she acted as the lead subject matter expert for the development of their Expert and Guru Certification training.

Judie is a Massachusetts native who now lives in Florida with her husband Bob. She enjoys the outdoors, watching football and is an avid New England Patriots fan.

# Index

CPSIA information can be obtained at www.ICGtesting.com
Printed in the USA
BVOW11s2341100515

399545BV00003B/4/P

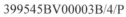

9 781942 417002